The Boy Who Was Born a Girl

One mother's unconditional love
for her child

Jon and Luisa Edwards

arrow books

Published by Arrow 2013

2 4 6 8 10 9 7 5 3 1

Copyright © Jon and Luisa Edwards 2013

Jon and Luisa Edwards
have asserted their right under the Copyright, Designs
and Patents Act 1988 to be identified as the authors of this work

This book is a work of non-fiction based on the life, experiences and
recollections of the authors. In some limited cases names of people, places,
dates, sequences or the detail of events have been changed [solely] to protect
the privacy of others. The authors have stated to the publishers that, except
in such minor respects not affecting the substantial accuracy of the work,
the contents of this book are true.

First published in Great Britain in 2013 by
Arrow
Random House, 20 Vauxhall Bridge Road,
London SW1V 2SA

www.randomhouse.co.uk

Addresses for companies within The Random House Group Limited can
be found at: www.randomhouse.co.uk

The Random House Group Limited Reg. No. 954009

A CIP catalogue record for this book
is available from the British Library

ISBN 9780099558248

The Random House Group Limited supports the Forest Stewardship
Council® (FSC®), the leading international forest-certification organisation. Our
books carrying the FSC label are printed on FSC®-certified paper. FSC is the only
forest-certification scheme supported by the leading environmental organisations,
including Greenpeace. Our paper procurement policy can be found at:
www.randomhouse.co.uk/environment

Printed and bound by CPI Group (UK) Ltd, Croydon, CR0 4YY

Each year 100 children and adolescents in
the UK are affected by gender dysphoria

*(This is the reported figure from GIRES
[Gender Identity Research and Education
Society] at the time of our documentary in
2009)*

Acknowledgments

My deepest thanks to all those parents with transgender children who shared their journeys and experiences with me, giving support and reassurance during my difficult days.

Luisa

Contents

Preface

My son Jonathan was born twenty years ago, as my daughter Natasha.

One evening, at the age of fifteen and through pain and tears, my daughter told me that she 'felt like a boy'. With those four words and in those few seconds, everything changed: I never expected my child to say those words; I did not have the child I thought I knew. My world had been turned upside down. How fragile our life is at times. At that moment I lost my daughter.

Our continuing journey together of my child's transition from female to male has taught me the importance of acceptance in this life.

Through my confusion, pain and loss, my son's courage and integrity has shown me that to love one's child is to love unconditionally.

Luisa

One
Beginnings

Jon: Childhood

I was born Natasha Alana Edwards on 4 November 1992, in Lima, Peru, in South America. I think my early life must have been at least as eventful as it is now, but like most people I can only remember snippets. I envy people with crisp memories of their early life – it must be so fascinating to open up one's memories and to wander into one's childhood again. But for someone who can't even remember where they put their keys five minutes ago, it's a rather different story. However, I do remember some things from when I was very young.

According to my mum Luisa I was one of the smallest babies on the ward, and was dubbed 'Pixie',

1

which remained my nickname for years. I had, as my mum puts it, delicate ears, which looked like pixie's ears, and eyebrows and lips that looked as if they had been painted. Despite my tiny body and sweet appearance, apparently I could scream louder than any of the other babies, and had an appetite to match (which, unlike my appearance now, hasn't changed). I only remember a handful of things from when I lived in South America as we left to go and live in England when I was around one. When I look through photos, images seem to spark something deep within me; I remember the sun and the garden and sitting and playing with my toys. I remember the hummingbirds as if they're not just one of my memories but have become a part of me.

Many people ask me if I am Peruvian when I tell them where I was born, but actually I am Nigerian, Spanish and Geordie. My origins really are a mixture of cultural backgrounds. My mother is mixed race; her mother is Spanish and her father is West African. She was born in Leeds and had one younger brother. Mum lived in Nigeria until the age of eleven, when she went to boarding school in England. I have never been to Africa nor had any contact with my Nigerian family apart from my grandfather (who I used to call my African granddad) who visited us occasionally. I have masses of aunts and uncles and cousins out in Spain, in the rural north of the country.

My father is the Geordie part of me. My dad grew up on a council estate in Newcastle, was a high-achieving student and through hard work and his intellect went on to study politics. My parents were polar opposites, socially and culturally, which did mean that members from both sides of the family had difficulties accepting their relationship. They met at university, eventually got married and then were posted by the Foreign and Commonwealth Office, or FCO, to Peru. My mum had a rather exciting job there doing something against South American drug traffickers for Customs and Excise. I know, from asking when I was very young, that it involved coded messages, which was all I took in at that age.

When Mum and I moved back to England we initially stayed in Newcastle with my grandparents while Mum found somewhere for us to live by ourselves. My father finished his posting a few months later and then joined us. I vividly remember opening presents of cuddly toys on Christmas Day at my grandparents' house when I went back to visit them later on in my childhood. I loved stuffed animals, the fluffier the better. I was obsessed with rabbits and used to make them beds in my grandma's dresser cupboard. Soon after staying here we moved to a suburb of south-east London, along with my mother's mum, my Spanish grandma who I referred to as 'Lala'. I still live there now. The house is a medium-sized semi-detached in a quiet area, with a nearby park, playground and school, and is only a ten-minute walk from the high street. The back garden backs on to a small alleyway, which is more of a dirt track overshadowed by trees that links all the garages together. In the front garden stands a huge tree, marking the corner of the street. Out of my bedroom window I can see the wood that encloses the park. I'm thankful for being brought up near trees and greenery. As a child, I was often taken for long walks in the park and the woods by my mum and grandma. From my early life, I remember the house undergoing renovations and extensions. At one time, there was a black painted metal gate and a stony pathway leading from the front garden to the back. I remember it smelling rather unpleasant – metallic, and slightly of stale smoke. I remember that Lala's bedroom used to be a living room with colourful sofas but the curtains were heavy and it was often dark. At one stage my bedroom was painted a yellow colour with *Lion King* stickers around the mirror, then it became blue with an ocean-themed design and now it's purple and silver.

The playschool I went to was a short distance down the road, and I still remember the path I took to get to it. The concrete was cracked by the huge roots of oak trees, which sprouted oddly from the pavements near the hall, making riding my tricycle or scooter to and from the building tricky but exciting. In my grandma's room, which is now a spare room, there's a picture of me on my first day of pre-school. I remember this photograph being taken very clearly. I was introduced to the teacher and she positioned me against the wall to get my photo taken for the class. In that picture it's all there – my round (or, as my grandma called it, 'moony') face smiling, chubby and cute, my rosy pixie lips and olive-toned skin. I was a messy young girl with short curly hair, and in the photo I'm wearing pink dungarees. I don't remember what happened after that but I remember those pink dungarees, and I remember feeling very small.

At playschool one of my favourite activities was raiding the dressing-up box as soon as I got there. I adored dressing up as a child (and I still do now!) and at every opportunity swapped my everyday clothes for something beautiful and magical. My favourites were a fairy and a princess outfit, and my mum has told me how she would always see me riding around on one of the tricycles all dressed up. I can recall lots of snow during my childhood – snow that I saw regularly at Christmas and not just during March or other odd months like we see it now. I would build huge snowmen with Mum, using black winter bark for buttons and a carrot for a nose. During one of those winter months I remember my buggy collapsing on the way to the doctor's surgery when Lala was pushing me.

When at the age of five I started reception at the local infants school, it was short lived, because my family was moved to Saudi Arabia on another posting. My grandmother meanwhile stayed and looked after the house. We were over there for about two years. We moved to the capital Riyadh, where they had a vast compound for diplomats. I changed from the woolly hats and gloves that I'd been used to in England to light summer dresses and shorts, and replaced the green bushes back home with sitting underneath the palm trees which grew in the dry orange earth of our front yard. The pristine, cool walls of the compound kept out the desert heat and cut us off from the dust storms outside. The house felt like a palace with its huge gates at the entrance to the compound at the side of the arid road. It was overshadowed by a neglected park, which housed a jungle of unused steel playground equipment which none of the kids ever got to play on as it was rarely open.

I remember well significant events from this time, such as getting my bottom row of teeth pulled out – apparently I had too many. Afterwards, for being brave, Mum took me out to buy a present. I had a choice between a video of *The Lion King II* or a pink, pouffed princess dress with long white gloves and a tiara. There was no contest: pink dress won hands down.

In Riyadh, the children of diplomats went to an English-speaking school. Looking back at that time in my life, I now see and understand the stark contrasts: the high-class, vast, shiny school you could get lost in and where there were only white faces to be seen, and having maids at home, while they and their families lived in cramped, dark flats an hour away. For two years I lived with the privilege of a big television, whatever food I wanted, tennis lessons and swimming at the pool.

Despite this privileged lifestyle, it wasn't all great living in Saudi. It was around this time that my parents started to spend more and more time apart, and I remember sensing that their relationship was becoming strained and cold. I was either with my mum or with my dad and I rarely remember them being in the same place at the same time. I don't remember any affection shown openly between them. I don't think my dad was a very affectionate person, and I don't recall him displaying any love for my mum. However, the brunt of the breakdown of my parents' relationship was for the most part kept away from me, and I was in my own little world in my room with my Spice Girls tapes and dressing-up clothes.

What friends might not know about my childhood

was that I stopped eating properly when I lived out in Saudi; in fact, I developed bulimia at a very young age. It's not something I feel the need to talk about much as I don't regard it as having a long-term effect on me. I must have been about six or seven when I became quite ill. I used to spit out my food in the toilet and refused to eat full meals entirely. My mum has since told me that it took me about an hour to eat a small pot of yoghurt, and even then she needed to feed it to me. This is strange, as eating disorders are more commonly associated with older children and teenagers rather than younger children.

To find the roots of my aversion to food I was taken to see an American psychiatrist. After spending a number of sessions drawing my feelings on paper (I didn't talk much during our sessions) he diagnosed my problem as an emotional reaction to the break-down of my parents' relationship and the increasingly intense arguments that they were having. I don't remember having any particular feelings about my parents' marriage falling apart, but I do remember starting to become afraid of my father's temper. He always flared up very easily and, while I don't like to admit it, I believe I may have inherited some of his temper. I don't feel that he dealt well with my bulimia; he got angry when I didn't eat and shouted at me for wasting something he'd cooked and that I said

I wanted. I always preferred eating with Mum; she would be kinder. I once took some horrible medication, and spat it out on the kitchen counter and he went ballistic.It seemed to me to be the little things that set him off and I was very wary to do anything around him in case I was wrong. There were times I didn't even feel like being around him.

The psychiatrist must have done something right as I gradually started eating properly. This episode, which lasted about a year, doesn't affect my life now. Although I am still very slim, my appetite is normal. Did I have a happy childhood out in Saudi though? Yes, I did. There was nothing particularly bad about it, and my bulimia seemed to have no marked effect on my mood, as far as I can remember.

Sonia, my lovely Filipino maid (I called her my 'Filipino angel'), would take me round to her flat some afternoons when I returned from school and Mum was still at work. I loved playing with the children in her compound and being with her loved ones. She felt like part of our extended family, and always invited me round for birthday parties and at Christmas. During one of these times I remember dancing to nineties music and playing a game of pass-the-parcel under disco lights in a dingy hall. Standing outside of the apartment block in which she lived were trees that I used to climb with the other boys – one time I fell off backwards and discovered to my horror the ground underneath was home to a fat albino slug. Another time, she taught me to ride on a bicycle which was far too big for me. I got my big toe caught in the chain and crushed the nail. Not a particularly fond memory: I was standing crying in the bathtub of my house while she hosed the blood from my foot and put iodine on it. Luckily it wasn't anything serious. I enjoyed her company and her presence bustling around the house was comforting. She kept the house in Riyadh immaculate and made the best pancakes rolled up with jam, sugar and lemon.

I had a best friend out there who was the child of another diplomat and went to the same school as I did. I can't remember her name, but she had blonde hair, very blue eyes, was in the same class as me at school and enjoyed watching the same Disney films as I did – like *Basil the Great Mouse Detective*, a particular favourite. I think I had a crush on her, even at that early age, and throughout our friendship I always viewed myself as a 'boy' in relation to her. Her parents would take us both on trips into the *wadi*, a rocky desert landscape about an hour away from our house where dust storms would whip up and you could walk for hours in the bleached stone lands. When we zoomed away from a dust storm in the back of a 4x4 we pretended we were a prince and princess escaping from desert bandits, imagining that the cars behind us were chasing us as we looked out on them. I remember her house was very grand and much bigger than mine, with rich hanging tapestries, marble bathrooms, lush rugs and huge stairs. I used to spend a lot of time lounging around there watching movies, looking at the Arabian items her father had collected, which included a polished wooden game with lots of balls, and eating snacks of apple and cheese while perched on the huge arm of one of the living-room sofas.

The only thing I didn't like about Saudi was when my mum used to wear the hijab, a loose black tunic-like garment, outside the confines of our compound; it unnerved me that I couldn't see my mum's face underneath her black headscarf. I also remember the little things, like finding a pretty bauble at a local market for Christmas one day while I was out and having about ten pet fish and two tortoises I named Holly and Jay, after some children back in my reception class in England whose names I liked. After I had decided on their names I found out that the tortoise I had named Jay had a little J-shaped marking on its shell, and the one I had named Holly had an H. I looked after them very well and I remember cleaning and feeding them. Sonia looked after them when we moved back to England.

When I was seven, Mum decided that we should all move back to England as her and Dad's relationship was getting too strained. Mum had also been ill for a while after she came down with a severe case of chicken pox, which she caught from me. We moved back into our old house in south London with Lala. Life carried on as normal and I had very little trouble adjusting to my old way of life. I went back to the same primary school, and although I barely remembered the people in my old class I quickly made friends again. I was happy to leave my strange early life – the camels on the motorway and luxurious compound – behind me.

Shortly after we returned to the UK, my father moved out of the family home. He would come and take me out on weekends to London or to the nearby park. We had a good relationship after him and Mum split up, for a while at least.

In between my normal everyday life in England there were holidays to Spain. I had always enjoyed playing princess for my Spanish family in a pink flamenco dress and with my ears pierced I could complement the outfit with beautiful hoop earrings. I aspired to look like my gorgeous older cousin, Raquel, who was a tall, athletic girl with long brown hair. My Spanish family always said she was the older version of me and I took this to mean that I needed to be as good as her when I grew up, if not better. My Spanish great-grandmother had a lot of children, and being a staunchly Catholic family, they in turn had a lot of children themselves! To this day I still don't know the names of all my relatives, or how many I actually have, and I only see them very occasionally. I did see them more when I was younger, when my grandmother on my mother's side was still alive, but since she passed away some years ago, I've only visited Spain once or twice. I remember one of the times I visited for a cousin's wedding when I was around thirteen. I tried a cigar offered to me by an older jolly relative and was also allowed to drink, which I found exciting. I remember at the reception afterwards having a big crush on the good-looking husband of one of my cousins; his name was Gabriel and his beauty was model-like. In Spain, the custom is to kiss in greeting on both cheeks, and needless to say, I did it with gusto.

Apart from living in Peru and Saudi my early childhood was a very 'normal' one. Nothing whatsoever to suggest any inner boy, nothing out of the ordinary from any other little girl's childhood. I played with 'girls' toys' as well as 'boys' toys', and my mum didn't try and force anything on me. I was who I was: Natasha, a girl who liked pretty things but also rough and tumble with her dad, when he was around. Though my mum didn't try to dress me up the way she wanted me to look, my grandmother always liked to see me in dresses and girly things as she had always wanted a girl for a grandchild. I only started to mind being put in a dress when I got to primary school – and that was nothing to do with being uncomfortable with my gender, it was so I could join in and play games with the boys. However, I soon decided it was much more practical to wear dresses than trousers in summer because of the heat. And besides, I often wore PE shorts underneath my dress like most of the girls. But playing with boys' toys and being a tomboy is certainly not an indicator of *feeling* like a boy. I was happy being only a tomboy back then; I knew that other people saw me as one of the girls. I could see other girls and recognise I was part of their group at the end of the day, no matter how much I socialised with the boys. At that time I didn't feel 'in the wrong body', and I didn't question or feel unhappy when I got my first period – which came in late primary school at the age of ten. At that age I just didn't think about biology or what made me different. I knew I wasn't your stereotypical girly girl, but I didn't question my gender.

To be clear, gender and sex are not interchangeable terms. Your sex refers to the sexual organs you have at birth, but your gender is whether you think of yourself as male or female. People whose assigned sex at birth does not align with the gender they believe themselves to have are said to have 'gender dysphoria'.

Plenty of cis women (people who are happy that the female sex assigned to them at birth matches their mental gender) were, or still are, tomboys. Indeed, many transgender men use the excuse 'oh, I was such a tomboy when I was younger' in order to validate their gender identity to a cissexist (the belief that the genders of trans people are less legitimate than those of cis gender people) society. Even I, someone who hates simplifying my experiences to fit the norm, have talked about my childhood in this way, as though I need to have evidence to suggest why I am transgender. In many ways, to be taken seriously as a man, trans men feel they need to 'butch up' their pasts, saying that they knew from age zero that they were boys, lest their identities be dismissed as false. I didn't know how I felt at an early age in regards to my gender; I just knew I was set apart from the other girls in what I liked to do, and I fitted in better with the boys.

I enjoy talking to other people about this part of my childhood, especially parents of other young trans people. It's a widely held misconception that all trans people's childhoods are very much alike, that there are set signs and indicators in the toys trans people played with as children, or the clothes that they wore, that meant they would 'grow up to be trans'. But this is a common misconception that isn't borne out in reality. Trans men don't have to have played football and wrestled with other boys when they were growing up and trans women didn't have to play hairdressers and carry Barbie dolls, just like cis people don't. Just because we are trans doesn't mean we have to conform to gender stereotypes. We are just as diverse as any cis person in our gender presentation. Feminine trans boys exist, and there are plenty of butch trans girls. I particularly enjoy talking to parents about this in order to break any preconceptions or misinformation they may have about what is a 'typical' trans person.

Of course, there are many who do fit the stereotype, and those are the stories that you usually hear about or read; the children knowing from the outset that they had been born with the 'wrong bodies' and feeling confused as to why other people can't see them for the gender they truly believe they are, not understanding why they are not allowed to wear a skirt with their uniform, or why they can't use the boys' toilets like all the other boys. I know some younger children who attend the UK support group Mermaids – a group for young transgender people and their families – feel this way, and if you read these children's stories or look at their pictures of how they see themselves you often get an impression of the isolation and the confusion they face from others but also from themselves.

It's also important for me to point out that even in cases where children 'act like the opposite gender' in childhood, it may just be a quirk. They may grow out of it; they may just like that stuff. It's also worth pointing out that where it's OK for girls to be tomboys and play with boys' things, if boys want to wear pink and dress up as fairies it's often seen as wrong and as an indication that the child obviously must be either gay or a young trans girl. Our society, which values masculinity over femininity, rears its sexist head.

I have seen that when boys play with girls' toys and dress up in girls' clothes, they are bullied at school. This happened recently to the child of a friend of mine. When she brought it up with her son's teacher it was suggested that the bullying was her son's fault for being too feminine. The teacher said to my friend that if she wanted her son to stop being bullied she must buy him boys' toys, suggesting that his behaviour was effeminate and not the norm. To my knowledge, this is not a rare case, in fact, it is a disturbingly frequent occurrence for some teachers to blame children and parents for something they can't help, to victimise them for their gender presentation or for being open about their sexuality. And when *young* children (he was five) and their parents are forced to deny or dampen down parts of their personalities because of other people's prejudices it is an injustice. This teacher implied that such a child deserved to be bullied. My friend's child may be trans when he grows up, he may not. He may be gay, he may not. He may be bisexual, he may not. He may be many things. But whatever he identifies as later on in life, his childhood needs to be safe and happy. He's a child, and children should have the right to express themselves freely; after all, enough constraints will be placed on them as adults. Sadly, these constraints are often set up in places (such as, sometimes, a classroom) where conforming to a set of gender stereotypes is seen as desirable. However, it seems obvious to me that in a classroom environment stereotypical views should not be the only ones that are available. These views do not represent the diversity of life.

I find that talking about gender-variant young children to people often shocks and confuses them, even people who consider themselves fairly open-minded. The subject of young children being transgender can make them feel very uncomfortable. This shows how taboo this subject still is, in that young children can't freely consider themselves to be another gender. But is it abnormal? I mean, when does anyone first do gendered things? Two, three or four, maybe before that? When did you first play with a Barbie doll or an Action Man? When did you decide which colours of clothes you liked? For some children, there is an incongruence between what their parents say they are and what they feel they are. When a gender is expressed at a young age through telling someone or by displaying stereotypical gender roles like playing with Barbies or dressing up in pink dresses, then it is more noticeable. But not every child will do this.

Some kids know from a very early age that something is wrong with how other people see their gender, but some trans people discover this later in life. The fact is that when many older people hear children or even teenagers talking about feeling trans or gender-variant or questioning, they automatically dismiss it as a phase. Like I say, quite often this is just because of their age but crucially sometimes their age isn't a factor. In most cases of people not feeling like the gender they were assigned at birth, they've had this experience for a long time before they've been able to say it out loud. They've mulled over it, questioned it, researched and pondered their feelings. Only when we feel fairly certain will we come out, or tell another person. This was how it was for me, in any case.

However, as you can tell from the accounts my childhood, I wasn't a stereotypical young boy but nor did I have gender dysphoria when I was very young. In the way I looked and what I played with, I went from one extreme to another. One day I would want to only do boys' things, another day I was happy going to a friend's birthday party in a new dress. Mostly it was the more feminine presentation that I adhered to in my early childhood.

When I started to transition in my mid-teens, I felt at home in my own skin enough to draw on the child that I was and to embrace the feminine part of me. Was my early feminine presentation something of the raging queer guy coming through? I like to think it may have been!

At infants' school, which in my town was directly linked onto the primary school, I dressed as a female. I wore dresses in the summer and I remember loving the costumes that my grandma, a brilliant seamstress, made me for the days when you could dress up as your favourite historical figure or book character. Gender never seemed to be an issue at that time.

When I moved onto primary school I was a 'tomboy' pretty much constantly, which is a distinct change from how I had been any time before at school. I now hated the summer dresses that I had once loved so much! I got on well with boys, who made up the majority of my friends, and I had quite a few girl friends; everything was fine. I definitely considered myself a geek, I got on with my work and preferred to speak to the teachers rather than my peers. I loved reading and literacy lessons, although I learned to hate maths with a passion in Year 3 when I had a very harsh teacher, who totally destroyed my confidence in that area.

During my time at primary school my weekends were very varied: I went to the park down the road with friends and round to their houses to play games, but on the whole I was quite a solitary child. I played my Game Boy by myself in my room and went on the Internet and generally kept myself to myself. I was hooked on listening to audio books and reading, having discovered Tolkien and *Harry Potter*, who was a huge part of my childhood and I still have a deep love for this series today. Reading that fired my imag-ination, making being on my own in the world of Middle-earth or Hogwarts perhaps more enjoyable than the world outside my bedroom. On weekends my father would visit and take me out for the day in central London, where we would go to the London Dungeons, museums or the cinema. On the whole, I was a fairly happy child.

I noticed that everyone started to become more gender conscious between the ages of nine and eleven, as they started to reach puberty. This is when I started to get hassled. As I said before, I didn't feel

I identified with the other girls. I didn't want to do the things that they wanted to do and while I did have a few girl friends to begin with, in the end I didn't speak to them, and they didn't speak to me. But I was fine with this social exclusion – I had the boys to play with and I was happy with that. However, I began to feel like I didn't fit in anywhere. I was a girl, I accepted that I was one because I was told I was, but I didn't see why I had to do just girls' things. Unlike my peers, I couldn't see that I was different – I was simply me. I was playing the games I wanted to play and talking about the things that I wanted to talk about. Looking back, I can see this as deferring from the binary gender system (the system that only has male and female as gender options), not just being a tomboy. However, I didn't identify as a boy back then as some young trans kids may do. I didn't identify as anything. I could see that I wasn't a 'biological boy' and for years I just accepted that fact.

But I refused to wear a dress in primary school or do anything stereotypically girly, which looking back at my early childhood is quite a surprise. I think it was a reaction to the social exclusion I was facing because of the activities I wanted to do. As my classmates and I started to approach puberty, I wasn't accepted in the girls' circle of friends, so I didn't have to take care of my appearance or dress up nicely and the boyish clothes I wore were far more practical anyway. I was always being pushed to wear a dress by my grandma who wanted me to look pretty, but I was more comfortable dressed down in tracksuits and sweatshirts, with my unruly head of curls. I thought that the boys would treat me differently if I came to school wearing a dress; it would be so different from what they would usually see me in and I wouldn't be treated as an equal as they always had done before. Wearing girls' clothes would mean I would have to acknowledge my girly-ness, would somehow prove that inextricably I was still linked to the girls in another part of the playground. But they were everything I was not: they fitted in with other girls and didn't like weird things like fantasy books or playing fighting games like I did. Somehow, the way they acted was 'correct', and the way I acted wasn't.

People started to notice I wasn't acting in the way the other girls did and began, as kids do, to say nasty things about me. They wouldn't come near me, saying I had 'the lurgy' (a fictitious disease all the geeks and outcasts had, which made them 'untouchable'). There were a handful of girls who made nasty comments to me on a regular basis, but I got the impression that the majority of the girls in my class thought I was just odd and weird. I wasn't included in their activities and I wasn't spoken to. I had nothing to talk about with the other girls, which made me an outsider. I was actively made an outcast and it become a vicious cycle: the more they bullied me the more I hung around with the boys, and by hanging around with boys, the less of a 'girl' I became and the more they bullied me. And still, I couldn't see anything wrong with how I was behaving. I was just being me. Yes, I liked different things to the majority of the girls in my year, but I couldn't see how this was making them think I had some disease that meant they had to keep away from me. During this time Mum stepped in to talk to the teachers about this victimisation, but it didn't help much.

I've never been one to show outward signs of sadness at my bullying, even when it got particularly bad in secondary school. I've always wanted to deal with it by myself and not trouble anyone else. I don't like other people worrying about me. I'm a 'motherly' person; I like taking care of people and making sure that other people are OK, going as far as not taking care of my own problems and hoping that they would sort themselves out on their own. I don't know when this developed, but I'm sure that I wouldn't have willingly told my mum that I was being bullied, I'm sure she would have had to dig that fact out of me. I also think there was a sense of embarrassment, even at that age, about why I was being picked on: I wasn't a normal girl. And nobody likes abnormal girls.

I was sad inwardly though and I had begun liking boys, which was terrible because I fancied some of my close male friends. They liked the attractive girls, not me who always wore trousers and had short hair and looked like one of them. I wanted to go out with a boy, a boy who could make me feel like a girl as no one else did. A boy who would find me pretty, who would help me be normal and, if I behaved normally, maybe I would stop being hassled every day. But nothing happened, no boys were attracted to me and they chose the other girls instead. I wasn't surprised; I was just frustrated and saddened.

In Year 6, the end-of-year trip to France was slowly looming and I was dreading it. No girl wanted to share a dorm with me, and anyway I wanted to share a room with my guy friends, the only real friends I had. This wasn't allowed, obviously, and I had to share with some of the girls whom I vaguely knew. Overall it was OK, because there were mixed-sex activities and I could hang out with the boys. But on the last day there was a disco.

Some of the girls in my dorm (not the ones who'd actively been nasty to me but the ones who had shown a wary indifference towards me) wanted to change me. I know their intentions were good. *Everyone* knew I was unpopular and a tomboy. For quite a while leading up to this point I had reasoned that to feel good and included, and to perhaps make myself more attractive, I had to wear some nice clothes, instead of the T-shirt and tracksuit bottoms that I lived in day in and day out. I honestly didn't mind dressing up – in my early childhood I always liked dressing up – so it was fine to wear some more 'hip' clothes for a change.

I had bought myself some nice feminine clothes: a fashionable (in the noughties) blue belly top, slashed diagonally in the middle, and tight jeans that laced up at the sides. When I put them on, the girls said I looked really nice. It was so good to hear compliments from them instead of silence, and for the first time I thought that I was doing something right. After they saw my outfit, they taught me how to walk, and told me what to talk about if anyone talked to me (*not* the *Lord of the Rings*, but Justin Timberlake would be OK). I felt awkward and unnatural, like riding a bike for the first time, but I assumed it would help me to become girlier, and to become liked in the end.

It didn't work, and apart from compliments on my appearance nothing really changed: I was still me, awkward and alone. The girls didn't talk to me after I reverted to my old self. I ended up hanging around the boys at the party and didn't make much of an effort to talk and walk differently. I just mucked around, and didn't dance with anyone or stand in a corner with the girls and talk. I got on the coach back to England the next day feeling no different from how I felt before the disco.

But this was the start of a new phase in my thinking. In my mind I could see the tomboy dying as I fought for acceptance with my own gender. The clothes I wore for the disco had made me somewhat attractive as a girl, as opposed to the baggy clothes I usually wore. I knew that going into secondary school, which was mere months away, I had to fit in. I didn't want to drag my awkward, frumpy, boyish self into that place and be treated in exactly the same way by other girls. I needed to make a conscious decision to change who I was, or risk being unhappy and bullied for years to come.

Luisa: Little hummingbird

It's hard talking about a past that now seems so removed from the present. Difficult because in my memory it is as though I had twins and have since lost one. But in reality I only ever had one child, a daughter I called Natasha.

As a parent you subconsciously map out your child's future and you do this thinking not about what they may want, but about your own aspirations and hopes for them. Hopefully us parents quickly learn to understand that this is about our own selfish needs, but it's all too easy to map out the life you want for them, rather than listening to their dreams. So with our own hopes and aspirations in mind, as our children grow up we try to steer them towards that future. In doing so we forget about their own individuality, one of the most important aspects of our children. I fell into this trap: I had assumed that my daughter would have a good career, be happy, maybe get married someday and have a family, all the usual things that parents hope for and as our children grow up we try to steer them towards that future. But this was about what I wanted. At times when I look at Jonathan today and I'm reminded of Natasha I do experience a painful and confusing sense of loss. The reality is I never had a daughter. I had a child who should have been born a boy. This fact would take us both on a very unexpected journey in life.

I never thought of myself as having maternal instincts. I remember telling my mother at the age of eleven that when I grew up I would adopt, especially when a school friend at the time told me what she had recently learnt about the process of getting pregnant. With a great deal of description she told me, in no uncertain terms, that it took at least six hours to get pregnant and you had to lie very still!

In all naivety I believed it to be true and so did she. At eleven my reaction was how yuck is that and I made a firm decision that I would avoid the 'yuckiness' and adopt. By the age of thirty my views on 'yuck' had changed.

My husband and I had been married a couple of years and the time felt right. I planned my pregnancy with great precision. Looking back now I realise that I was the one who decided it was time to start a family. Nat's father wanted the pregnancy too but not as intensely as I did. I remember the exact date of her conception, Friday 14 February 1992, Valentine's Day. We had celebrated with some bubbly and after a weekend of feeling the obvious hormonal changes of being slightly nauseous I was sure that I was lucky enough to be pregnant. Two months later the doctor confirmed this. I was so happy.

I had a textbook pregnancy with none of the drawbacks of morning sickness, swollen ankles, bad indigestion and all the other discomforts that pregnancy can bring. I loved being pregnant. I looked as though I had swallowed a watermelon; I had a perfect round little bump. I remember my Spanish grandmother saying that was the safest place to be, inside, warm and protected.

Whilst at one of the routine pregnancy scans with my husband the doctor told us the sex of our baby.

The scan was recorded and I still have those blurry images of my child in my womb. Dr Prazak said it was a boy, then after a few more minutes declared 'No, it's a girl, definitely a girl.' I was happy, especially because my mother so wanted a little girl. How excellent, how perfect to give her a granddaughter. To know for definite that it was a girl. There was to be no definite from that scan onwards. My daughter was born at 1.15 a.m. on 4 November 1992.

I had been in labour for most of the day before without really realising. By the evening, as my contractions intensified, we made our way to the maternity clinic, an extraordinary journey in itself. At the time, my husband and I were working at the British Embassy in Lima, Peru, and due to increased terrorist activity the government had declared a state of emergency and imposed a curfew. So we drove to the clinic with the lights on in the car, occasionally being stopped to have our carnets checked at various military security points. By the time we arrived I was fully dilated and ready to give birth. It was intense, painful, quick and amazing.

I remember the nurse bringing her to me once I had been settled in my room. Natasha Alana Edwards. We chose the name Natasha because it means birthday and given if you are born close to Christmas. It also has Russian origins. Alana means 'precious; awakening' in Old German and Hawaiian. It felt right to choose a name that reflected her cultural diversity – a United Nations baby. My daughter was tiny, weighing under six pounds. The nurse said, 'Señora, she is the only girl in the maternity unit, she is the smallest of all the babies here but she sure has some lungs on her!' Nat was the only girl born that day, surrounded by eight-pounder plus boys in the baby unit. The nurse said that as soon as she started crying, because she was hungry, she caused a domino effect and set the rest off. It makes me smile thinking about that; that was my girl, born into the world small but making her presence known. My mum called her 'little hummingbird' as she reminded her of the beautiful tiny hummingbirds that would come and hover around the flowers in our garden in Peru. My pet name for Natasha was 'Pixie', as she had tiny pointy ears and looked as though she had been painted. Because her birth had been so quick and without trauma she was not bruised or swollen. She had the most perfectly shaped eyebrows, little pink cheeks, a tiny button nose and rosebud lips. She looked as though the fairies had left her as a gift – my little pixie.

My mother came over to Peru a month before Nat's birth and stayed with us for four months. It was important for her to be there and she was a tremendous support, caring and totally in love with her granddaughter. Once I had stopped breast-feeding she took over, waking up every few hours during long and tiring nights to bottle feed our Pixie. When Natasha was just a few weeks old, Mum would take her out to our little front garden in her cot pram when the heat of the day was turning into warm afternoon, placing her pram in the shade but making sure that her little legs got the fading sunlight. 'It will make her legs strong,' she would say. I remember going away for a break with a friend to Machu Picchu in Peru. I was away for less than a week and called Mum every day. On one of these occasions she excitedly related to me Natasha's first time eating solids. She said that she reminded her of a newly born baby bird in its nest, beak wide open, eager and hungry, she couldn't get the little spoon with the puréed fruit in her mouth fast enough. How important it is, I realise now, to remember memories and moments like that.

When Mum left to go back to work in London I had Maura our housekeeper to help me out. She lived outside Lima with her son, daughter-in-law and two granddaughters. She was in her mid-fifties but looked much older, due to the fact that she had worked very hard all her life.

It does make me feel uncomfortable saying

'our housekeeper'. It sounds colonial, born out of unnecessary privilege, but the fact is we did have a privileged lifestyle. We had a beautiful house built into the surrounding rocks next to the ambassador's residence, all set in a gated compound. There were formal functions, dinners, poolside lunches, security guards, chauffeurs, maids, nannies and gardeners, all part of the diplomatic lifestyle.

Even though Maura was employed as our housekeeper the relationship we developed was one of mutual respect and closeness. To me she was my Peruvian grandmother. She cared for and loved Natasha like one of her own. I remember the first time she saw little Pixie and said to me, with great affection, '*que miseria*'. The literal translation is 'what a tiny creature'. It became her mission, once Natasha was on solids, to feed the tiny creature and feed her she did. She was an amazing cook and from the age of four months Nat was having garlic in her puréed vegetables. (To this day Jon enjoys all kinds of foods and flavours as a result of no-fuss eating from an early age.) Maura used to take Nat for walks around the compound in her arms, stopping to show her off to the security guards. Once Maura said to me, 'Thank you, señora, for trusting me with your child.' I was surprised by her words; she explained that some of the families she had worked for only ever treated her as the hired help. That truly saddened me. It showed me how privilege perpetuates negative stereotypes about people less fortunate than us. I am grateful and thankful to have had her care, support and friendship during my time in Peru. The day Nat and I left Lima Maura did not come to say goodbye; we had said our goodbyes hastily the day before. It would have been too difficult for us both to say them any other way.

As a baby Natasha was happy and full of energy, always wide-eyed and learning. I have an amazing photograph of her at just six weeks old, lying on the bed about to be changed. She's on her stomach and has pushed herself up as though she is about to do press ups, her little neck and head straining upwards in the air with a look of determination on her face. The photo reminds me of the lizards I used to see in my childhood in West Africa, as they would sit in the sun bobbing their heads up and down. I told the paediatrician about this at Natasha's next routine check-up and she was quite amazed. She said it was down to Natasha's sheer will because her tiny neck muscles were still developing to support the head. This will is what I see now in the courage of my son as he deals with his journey of transition.

We moved back to England after our three-year

posting abroad. Nat was around one and it was now time for nursery. Nat loved the interaction with other children, especially the boys. In her tracksuits she jumped, climbed, did roly-polys and a great deal of other rough-and-tumble activities, so it made sense to dress her in the most comfortable and practical of clothes. Dressed like this she could be free to play. Yet the first thing we had to do when the nursery doors opened was to make a beeline to the dressing-up rack and get the frilly pink ballet tutu! On it went, on top of the tracksuit, and she would then get on a blue-and-red tricycle and pedal away energetically. My little Pixie tomboy in a pink tutu.

Nat's early childhood was full of activities. I used to take her to 'Tumble Tots', which as the name suggests was an activity where tots could tumble! Once a week she would bounce on a trampoline, do roly-polys on soft colourful mats, walk across benches and generally have a great deal of fun and play with other 'tots' her age. As happy and outgoing as she was I remember there was one piece of equipment that Nat was not happy about. There was this accordion tunnel that the 'tots' would go through but, as adventurous as my Pixie was, the tunnel was not her thing. She would stick her head into the worm-like tube then quickly take it out again and just crawl round it to the next activity.

Eventually one day she decided that she would go through that colourful elasticated tunnel! Just like when she was learning to swim she loved being in the water but putting her head under was something else. All the other children in her swimming group would put their heads under but not Nat. Her swimming teacher said, 'She needs to do it in her own time,' and so it was. We would encourage her to just stick her nose into the water. It reminds me now of our kitten who still hasn't got to grips with drinking from her water bowl and dips her nose in too far and then has to do a series of little snorts as the water goes up her nose. She then hurriedly shakes her head and whiskers trying to get the water off! Nat would do the same: nose in, snorts and a hurried shaking of her head. And, in her own good time, one day she did put her head fully underwater.

Nat's childhood was surrounded with love and care. During the cold winter months 'Lala', our pet name for her grandmother (Lala in Peruvian means one who tends the little ones, more specifically, a name given to goat herders who protect and tend the kid goats), would wrap Nat up in warm layers, usually knitted bobble hats and woolly jumpers sent by her 'nana' (my ex-mother-in-law, who was an avid knitter). All trussed up in layers of wool Lala would take her down to the park. 'It's important for a child to get fresh air,' she would say and off they went, happy in each other's company. It was my mum who first introduced Pixie to swings. They both spent many a summer and winter in the park. They had many happy times together. Remembering this aches because my mother is no longer here. But I am grateful that the time they spent together brings back those memories of love.

Nat had a real joy for life, for expression, for laughter. She was an independent child, questioning and headstrong. A thinker, she read, drew and role played from a very early age, often on the carpet surrounded by figurines. These would range from dinosaurs to Sylvanian Families woodland animals with Nat making up stories and giving them different voices. There seemed to be a real need for expression in her. Looking back now I can see that her play was usually in a male role. She would earn pocket money by making salads to go with dinner, setting the table and waiting on my mum and me with a folded tea towel over her arm. She would serve us and leave little folded notes on the table saying, 'Jeeves hopes you enjoy. Please leave a tip.' I still have some of these tucked away in my drawers, along with home-made birthday and mother's day cards and little notes that she left on my pillow some nights. Nat saved up fifteen pounds in her piggy bank and went shopping with her dad one weekend, returning home clutching a large box. In the box was a Roman Centurion outfit, sword, helmet, chest-plate – she was so excited with her purchase. It did surprise me but then it also made sense: that was exactly what my tomboy of a girl would enjoy playing with.

Summer days were spent in the back garden, mostly with boy friends that she had made in infant school. She would make me tie a sheet around her shoulders as a makeshift cape. Centurion helmet and breastplate on with sword at the ready, she and the boys would re-enact battle scenes. They would have sticks for swords and their play involved lots of running and tumbling. Natasha was happiest playing with the boys. There was a connection there, an understanding of their world of play. Later in her life it would become apparent as to why she had such a natural understanding of boys and their world.

Nat loved acting and was very good at it. When she was eight she wanted to go to weekend stage school and she performed in local stage productions. She was always the first to jump into a boy's role. The girls, costumes were fabulous, especially for the opera productions she was in – corsets, beautiful petticoat dresses but my Nat wanted to be in breeches with a waistcoat and tricorne hat.

She loved reading and being read to. Her first

book (which I still have) was a small thick hardback with bright colours depicting letters of the alphabet. The usual A is for Apple alongside a picture of a bright red apple, B is for Ball and so on. There are teeth marks on some of the page corners where the book was used as a comfort to her teething gums. But I do remember that she would also hold that book in her plump little hands, turn the thick pages and look intently at the pictures. It would be the beginning of her great joy for the escapism that the written word and the world of books provides. Even now Jon still remembers some of the reading times we had together. *Owl Babies*, which tells the story of three baby owls that are scared and alone in their nest as mummy owl leaves them to find food, made a real impression on Jon. He has told me that at the time he was frightened and sad for the little owls as he worried that mummy owl might not be able to find her way back to them. The other story he remembers is *Little Polar Bear*, a story of a mother polar bear with her cub. She tells him of the wonderful icy landscape they live in as they look over the frozen sea. What is so touching about this story is their bond as mother and baby. As they look up at the Northern Star she tells him that she loves him like the ocean and back. Jon still remembers me telling him that too (and at times I still use those words), that I loved him like the ocean and back, and explaining that because the ocean wraps round the world it is endless, like my love for him. Our relationship has always been strong, a bond of security formed by always being there for my child, even though there were times because of a recurring illness that I have struggled to maintain this bond.

The night my daughter told me that she felt like a boy was the night I lost the child I thought I had. All my memories and experiences were those of bringing up a daughter. She was far from being a stereotypical 'girly girl', she was a tomboy, but she was still my girl. My initial sense of loss and confusion made me feel that everything I thought I knew about my child, the daughter I had, was not true, was invalid. The child I thought I had was not the same child that told me that they were in the wrong body, in a totally wrong gender casing. I am ashamed to say that I had no idea what transgender meant. How many of us would if it does not directly touch our lives? I thought it was to do with cross-dressing, being a transvestite. I certainly had no idea whatsoever that it is a recognised medical condition, that it is something you are born with, that it means that your brain gender is at variance with your body, the sex you are assigned at birth. There would be a lot of learning to do.

There was the pain of guilt that I had not seen this one profound and essential part of my child's being. There were initial feelings of inadequacy as a mother and parent. How could I not know the child I had? How could I have been so blind to something this big?

I know that Jon does not want to be referred to as 'she', he could never identify as a 'she', as a girl, as female. This makes me feel as though it's a betrayal to refer to him as she. We did an article for the *Guardian* newspaper (with Viv Groskop) and this was the first time that I heard Jon's true feelings on this.

JONATHAN: All trans people don't like their parents holding on to the person that they were.

LUISA: But you see there is a loss?

JONATHAN: Yes, but you have to understand: it's not a loss – it's a redefinition.

At the time I could not fully understand his feelings. I have slowly come to realise now that redefinition does not mean the loss of your child, it means that the child you had has become the person they should be. It still feels like a loss for many parents who have trans children, but accepting that it is still the same child only in a different definition has helped me in dealing with my feelings of loss.

There were painful moments where I felt I had let my child down. I know now that there is no blame to feel. How could I have known then, in her early years of childhood, something that Nat was still waiting to understand herself? How could I have known, before she herself could put it into words, that what felt so wrong to her was gender dysphoria? She was fifteen when she told me. Jon, my child who is now my son, is now twenty.

I realise now that Nat had always been Jon. She did not have to change that perception, she had always been a 'he', even though her external physicality said differently. I had to try and understand that fact. I have realised, and it is still at times an ongoing realisation, that 'my Nat' was always 'my Jon'. At the beginning, trying to make emotional sense of the situation left me with a conflicting mess of thoughts and feelings. Time is a healer and teacher, it has taught me that the conflicts I feel now will change as my understanding grows. The fact is that my son is now the person he was always meant to be. The journey of transition is one that we both have to take. As his mother I have my own mental and emotional journey of transition too. But my one constant in all of this is my unconditional love for my child. If at times my emotions felt very raw and difficult, what has always made sense and grounded me is this love.

I still find it so very hard to negate the daughter I once had. When I am remembering a childhood, Jon's past, I remember a daughter, my Nat, because she's part of my heart, my memory and my soul. I have a son now, but this son was once my daughter. For me, this daughter will always be part of Jon, but I'm beginning to accept that for him he was never a girl, ever. To him, Nat was this kind of stage persona. It was a performance, a shell.

Memories of Nat's childhood are very precious to me. Part of me still has a place for 'my Nat', although I feel that time may change that too. I am learning to reconcile my feelings of confusion to past memories. It helps if I can look back at the past in gender-neutral terms. Nat and Jon are one and the same and when it feels painful remembering a little girl then I remember a child – my child. That child never changed their core being. I had a son then too and in this acknowledgment I am remembering a childhood. Not Nat's, not Jon's, but the memories of my child's younger days. In doing this I remember the past in neither 'he' nor 'she' terms; this is my tool for understanding.

This is how I can best explain the way I feel. When

you go to see a film you suspend your disbelief, which makes you accept storylines, characters, situations that you would otherwise question if you constrained them within the limitations and barriers of an external world. For example, the law of gravity says that when you release an object, it falls to the ground. But in some films, the worlds that they create deny the existence of gravity. By suspending your disbelief, you allow yourself to see the film through the eyes of what is possible, not through those which can only see what is impossible. The suspension of disbelief makes you accept what you see on the screen because you do not limit your feelings or beliefs. While the external world has certain laws – such as the law of gravity – that most people accept as true, it also has a set of stereotypical beliefs – such as people's genders are fixed, not fluid – that sometimes we accept without thinking too much about them.

So when I rewind to my son's childhood I suspend my stereotypical beliefs by thinking outside of the box of what is and can only be that way. By not constraining my memories I do not have to place my child in a gender role of 'she'. My child then becomes their own person and not just a reflection of my beliefs and expectations; my child, this young person, who would later on in life undertake an essential, courageous and remarkable journey.

Although the feelings of loss are much easier to confront now, there are still moments that take me back to my memories of a girl with short curly hair running ahead of her mother on her way to school. A moment on the tube when I see a parent holding their young daughter's hand to steady her as they pull into the next station. Six-year-old boys in grey school shorts pedalling furiously on their bikes. Finding a Tupperware container in the back of the kitchen cupboard with NATASHA written on it in permanent black marker. They all remind me of my tomboy Nat and with sadness I think how different it could all have been for her if she had been physically assigned the right gender. I could throw that Tupperware container out, but for now keeping it feels part of my transition.

I still have many tangible memories of my daughter. Photos of Nat wearing a pretty dress to a birthday party; in her grey pinafore with her hair in a ponytail for her first day at primary school looking shy and uncomfortable. Her first ballet shoes; just as she loved to scramble up trees she loved to dance and took ballet lessons for a while. The first babygro she ever wore was bright pink and a gift from her uncle. I still have the tiny pink tag that was put around her wrist by the maternity nurse when she was born to denote her sex.

I know that letting go, which in reality means throwing out, is a difficult step for me. It feels as though I would be erasing part of my child and in doing that erase part of me. In some countries history is rewritten, chapters taken out of their history books, chapters added to suit the new reality, photos manipulated to present what should be seen. It makes me feel that throwing out these tangible reminders of my memories would be doing that too. Choosing to erase a past to suit the present. Her past is part of his present. Jon and I have spoken about photos of Nat and he has said that he is fine with some of them being kept and put into an album. We could have an album that is Nat as the tomboy that she was and have photos of Jon in there because visually there would be continuity. I could have a separate album that is about my Natasha? I don't know, I am unsure. Part of me wants to let go of emotional objects but then there is a part of me, the part that was the mother of Natasha, that wants to keep those images of a daughter.

Then I think, why keep photos of my daughter inside an album to share them only with myself? What I really want is to have an album of childhood to share with others. Photos of my child happily playing indoors, outdoors, standing wrapped up in layers next to their first snowman, dressed as Willy

Wonka for book day at school, in the park with his grandmother and the changing face and fashions of a young lad growing into his teens and becoming Jon. That is what is real and important to me.

Writing these words and re-reading them helps me make sense of conflicting feelings. It makes me remember a childhood that should not be based on a loss, but to remember a childhood that is about 'my child' who is now my son.

Last week I was walking on my usual route to work, which involves cutting through a small gated park. A tourist stopped me and asked if I could take a photo of him. I said, 'Sure, but I am not very good at taking photos so I hope it comes out OK.' I took one photo of him standing by a statue and was about to take another when a message came up saying that the battery was running low. I told him that I was sorry but could not take another one for him. He replied, 'Not a problem' and came over and looked at the digital image. 'That is fine,' he said. 'A photo is a moment in time and you have taken that moment, thank you.' With that we said goodbye. As I carried on walking to work I thought, I have just met a stranger who I will probably never see again yet he has given me something very important and essential without even knowing it. I thought of all the photos I have, from black-and-white photos of my mum in the sixties; the first photo ever taken of Nat in the delivery room; my brother and I when we lived in West Africa and many more. It made me realise that they aren't just images on paper but moments in time. Those moments are important in so many ways, they evoke feelings and sensations of a reality that was. I will look at photos very differently now and in doing so will not be saddened, but will try and remember all that was good and positive about that captured moment in time.

Letting go does not mean I forget Nat; letting go means remembering a present, my present life with my son. I know that I will take the difficult step I need to take, to let go and throw out certain tangible memories because I do not need to justify the love I have for my son with the love I had for Nat. What is essential has never changed: I love my son now as I loved my child then and that love has always been unconditional.

Two

Adolescence

Jon: Inside my mind

Was I faking it? It probably started out that way, but I grew to love being a 'girly girl' in secondary school.

Before I started school there was an open day to brief the incoming students on what they could expect and to meet some of the teachers. I knew one or two girls that I had got on with OK at primary school were going to be there, so I felt reassured that I wouldn't be completely on my own. I was determined that I would make a good first impression on prospective new friends and I felt I needed to put on a front, one of being chatty and sociable and great to hang out with.

When we arrived at the school hall where the open day was being held I sat with my friends from primary school who I had come with. The daughter of one of my mum's close friends who I liked and had known for a very long time was among them. I decided that I would copy them, I would laugh with them and I would even talk to new people, and crucially, I would talk to new people about the things that a 'normal girl' would talk about, not about anything weird or questionable. I felt OK, and soon began to feel comfortable in my new role, pleased that the other girls weren't seeing me as weird, and that I had the opportunity to impress them.

As far as I can remember, everything during the open day went perfectly. I talked to a lot of new girls – not boys, *girls* – which was new in my life. I remember I even went over to a girl sitting by herself and asked her to join our table! One girl called Sarah, who I talked to a lot, lived near me and we became good friends. It felt good to be talking to other girls after being ridiculed for socialising with boys all this time. It felt like I was doing something right.

Sarah and I, and my friends from primary school who had all chosen to go to the new school, decided that we would all travel on the bus together to our first day of secondary school in September. I felt like I was part of the *right crowd*. I was *one of them*.

Making a good first impression at the open day had been a success, and I was going to ensure this carried on, which it did. My first day of secondary school was uneventful, and I just blended in with all of the other girls. The new school was very near my house, but it hadn't been fully built yet, so Years 7 and 8 were in a white temporary build, which by the end was falling down around our ears. There was iron mesh on the windows and it felt very bleak looking out of them. The temporary build stood where the end of the playing field now is, and I remember sometime in November, under grey sky and drizzle, we had to trek up the field and dirt pathways to the great exoskeleton of the new school, which was just a lot of foundations, dirt and metal. We stood shivering where the hall was going to stand as the Bishop of Rochester said a few words about how wonderful the new school was going to be. It certainly didn't feel that way, and we just wanted to get back inside our little cabins to keep warm.

I made a real effort and began to read girls' magazines filled with gossip, make-up tips and fashion items. From being frumpy and antisocial in primary school, I quickly learned about music, clothes and what to talk about to other girls.

I asked for make-up for my birthday and Christmas. My mum was quite shocked at this extreme swing from tomboy to girly girl, but she didn't refuse me my choice in clothes or cosmetics, just like she had never tried to hide my previous masculinity. I had two huge boxes of make-up, full of eye shadow, blusher and lip gloss. I think I still have them in my cupboard some-where, they were so big I never finished using any of them. I used to sit in my room and try on various colour combinations to see which looked the best, and I planned my outfits for shopping or going to the cinema or ice-skating. I used to dress up, not as part of childhood games this time, but to try on outfits that I could wear out.

Although I wasn't in a form group with any of the girls who I had made friends with on the open day, I now knew socialising with girls was something I could do. In the beginning of Year 7 I made friends with mostly girls and hardly spoke to any boys. Once we got to know each other a bit more we went shop-ping together, and they came to my house and we talked about boys. Typical stuff, but it made me feel so secure in myself. There were a few boys in my friendship group, friends of friends, but at break times, instead of talking to them, I talked to the girls. I wouldn't get bullied – how *could* I get bullied? – as I was trying my hardest to be normal. It seemed to work, and I enjoyed my life as a girl. I enjoyed being pretty, and being seen as fashionable. So although it started out as a way to make up for my tomboy past, I genuinely enjoyed it. For the first time in my life I felt normal, and it felt brilliant.

What do I think of that time of my life now? Well, I could have done my make-up a bit better. And wasn't early noughties fashion terrible? But I don't look back in shame or embarrassment at what I liked because now, years on, I'm still as feminine as I was then! I suppose because of that fact it's not as hard for me as it may be for other trans men to see pictures of a time when they were obviously trying to present themselves as femininely as possible to negate the masculinity they felt. But when I think back to that time, I can only say that I enjoyed feeling pretty and good about myself, and that can't be a bad thing. The only real embarrassment I have looking back at those old photographs is how I looked in those clothes. I said on *The Boy Who Was Born a Girl* documentary that in one particular photo I looked, and I quote myself here, *'like a man in drag'*.

I feel now that was a very transphobic statement for me to make, and even more cringeworthy that I said it only a few years ago. It just shows how quickly people change. I'd like to take the opportunity here to take back those words and apologise. In embracing my feminine side now, two years on from the start of HRT (hormone replacement therapy), I can look back and say that at the start of my transition my masculinity was a bit of a farce, as it can be for a lot of trans guys. Without the physical effects of testosterone, one feels that one needs to shun anything that would hinder passing as male. This is what I did pre-testosterone, when I was starting to live as a trans man, and I think that is why I said what I said. I was rejecting my past when I was confronted so obviously with the picture of it in the documentary, a past that I was scared of associating with because of my early insecurities around not appearing male enough. In the picture I was referring to I looked so obviously female and my efforts with clothes and make-up were rather over the top. Drag queens (and kings) are beautiful and I don't feel that drag should be used as a word for something that you think is ugly. Drag, as I understand it, is to perform, to transcend boundaries. It is an art form and also a form of self-identification and a lifestyle many people have felt empowered by. Unfortunately, there is a certain amount of very negative feeling and even hate towards drag artists by so called 'real' trans people. As a minority, some transgender people feel drag performers are adding to the media's marginalising of trans people as fake men or women and that somehow they are insulting transgender identities. If I had used the word 'drag' in a context which meant my look in that particular photo was part of a performance, then I would not feel the need to write a long paragraph to clarify my words and reaction. Unfortunately, I don't think this is the way I meant it at the time.

Which makes me think: before I was introduced to the 'trans community' and other gender-variant people via the organisation Queer Youth Network, or QYN, what did I think 'trans' was? Did I even think? No, I didn't. I had no idea that if you were born one thing you could change to another, medically or any other way. I think I knew vaguely about male-to-female trans people but I didn't know (for lack of a better description) *what they were*. I had never been exposed to gender-variant or transgender people. I had no knowledge that this was a reality for some people. Unless we are directly or indirectly a part of a marginalised community, it's possible that any understanding we have about those communities is based on our ignorance. My secondary school's personal, social and health education was poor. Everything I learned about sexuality and exploring sexual identity I got from the Internet, like many teens do. I went to a school with a Christian ethos, which did not provide an educational space to talk about LGBTQ (Lesbian, Gay, Bisexual, Transgender, Queer) identities. Sadly, many schools do not include in their curriculum the essential need to openly discuss this issue of diversity and equality. Why I didn't come across anything mainstream on gender identity on the Internet, I'll never know. It seems like something should have sparked my interest, although I wasn't actively looking for anything. Also, I still identified socially as female at that point in my life, so I saw no reason to question that identity. Even if I had found information, I don't think I would have absorbed it.

In Year 8 I was beginning to drop the hyper-femininity of the previous year a bit, and relax my gender presentation more. My femininity gradually wore off as I started to talk to the boys in my friendship group more and branched out from the comfort zone of sticking to the girls. We played video games at break time and the façade that I had built up since leaving primary school began to drop. I ended up being bullied for who I was, just like in primary school. I started to hang out more with the boys and felt very comfortable talking to them without flirting with them and I was starting to gain more male friends. But I still retained the same female friends as I had before and I still liked make-up and still wore a skirt to school, even though you were allowed to wear trousers and some girls did.

So why then was I being singled out, yet again, for my gender presentation? Was it because of my fraternisation with the opposite sex? You'd think so, wouldn't you? But in reality I think it was more that I was outspoken. I wasn't afraid of voicing my opinion and I wasn't afraid of getting into confrontations, especially with boys. I was, in many ways, a strong female. As school is a melting pot of all sorts of insecurities, some of the other boys in school, especially the older ones, were embarrassed and uncomfortable at a woman being confident and 'unladylike', whereas I saw no problem with my 'masculine' behaviour. Because of my outspokenness and strong personality, I was often called a 'man', in a hateful and derisive way. I didn't class it as sexism back then but, looking back, of course it was. For being a strong young woman, I was called a 'beast'. I could not be a woman because, in their teenage minds, *female* was equated with being demure. I, who was not pretty, petite or quiet, had to be a 'freak'.

It was around this time that my mother became ill. She had, then undiagnosed, bipolar disorder and it came and went in episodes where she would be depressed for months at a time. I hadn't noticed it in primary school, and it was only when I started secondary school that I realised she was going to counselling and seemed to struggle for various periods of time. She would become withdrawn and unable to look after me, leaving me in the care of my grandma as she battled her depression.

She was drinking also and it was increasing in severity to the point where it affected my home life. One day I was waiting at the bus stop to go home from school and I received a call from a friend of Mum's. She told me that Mum been taken to hospital as she'd been drinking heavily from the morning. I tearfully asked if my mum was trying to kill herself. The friend said she didn't know. When I got to my bus stop I waited outside the supermarket for my mum's friend to pick me up and take me home. I rang up my grandma who was at work in London to tell her what had happened. She came back from work early to take care of me.

This incident really shocked me and I tried as best as I could to get on with my school life for that week while my grandmother took care of me. I was glad that Mum was out of hospital after a very short period of time and I just hoped it never happened again. A few years later, Mum spoke to me about this incident, about the guilt she felt at not being able to take care of me during those terrible periods because of her overwhelming depression and how she had tried to hide it for many years.

Meanwhile, the bullying at school had increased and was now happening every day. It had got so bad that I felt I couldn't walk down the corridor at school without the boys who were bullying me shouting something or making comments as I passed them. In the enclosed space of the temporary school, I couldn't escape their taunts. When we were moved to the main school building, the bullying carried on; whispers of who I was – a man, a freak, a beast – were passed down from year to year, from old student to new student. I wasn't targeted outside of school though, never around where I lived. There were some comments on the walk or the bus home. I preferred to walk home rather than take the bus and chance running into people who would harass me. The walk was about forty-five minutes, but I had my music for company. I didn't really get any of these comments from the girls. I think that for the boys I was somehow intruding on their masculinity and that threatened them, as it was something that they saw as theirs and theirs alone. The girls weren't too spiteful, but I think that they viewed me as an oddity and someone who they should not stick up for, or call their own.

I did have friends, the same group of friends that I had always had from the start of secondary school, so I didn't feel completely on my own. They didn't social-ise with the people bullying me so I felt safe around them. They weren't outcasts, but they weren't in the 'in crowd' either. I was comfortable in that circle; we were close knit, we shared similar interests and mostly kept ourselves to ourselves. I had always loved fantasy and creating my own worlds, so I wrote stories and poetry as a form of escapism and as a hobby. I projected a more confident, un-bullied and widely liked version of me on to the characters I made up, and enjoyed worlds of my own creation more than school life. This helped me through the bullying and feelings of isolation.

In those days I didn't identify as male, so there was no confusion or sudden epiphany when the word 'man' was thrown at me as an insult. It *was* absolutely an insult for me: my femininity had been broken and dismissed. The hard work, all my efforts to be viewed as a normal girl, was all for nothing.

I don't think the nature of the bullying changed my perception of gender. I understood that I was bullied because I wasn't like the other girls, but at the time I didn't think too much about the gender politics involved with being called a man. I just wanted to be a normal girl, and being called a 'man' in a derogatory way made me even more determined to reaffirm my identity as a woman. However, by this point I had reasoned that no matter what I did to conform, I would still be singled out as different in some way. I decided that I just didn't care any more if I did 'masculine' things or not. It was a really confusing time for me but I felt that whatever I did nothing would change this fact. The bullying in secondary school was done with such venom that I didn't care whether it was about my gender presentation or something else. Once again, it felt like I was being victimised just for being 'different'.

I suppose I socially identified as female because I didn't know anything else, and that seemed to be the identity I was 'meant' to flow with, for all its quirks and drawbacks. However, inside *me*, I don't think I identified as anything. I was at heart a neutral being and when I posted my poems or writing on the Internet, I was always neutral and didn't advertise my gender. However, I found it natural to get into the minds of men in my writing; I could easily take on the guise of male characters while I found it much harder to relate to any female characters or even write from a female's perspective. One of the things I liked best about writing was that I could just be myself; I didn't have to have a gender. But if I did, it certainly wasn't female. This fantasy maleness was acted out by characters I wrote about. I used to project my personality – or the personality I wanted – on to them, and in their bodies and minds I would live on in fiction, as happy as them, with a new lease of life, a perfect feeling. But I knew it could never truly be. It was writing, role play and fantasy. Longing to live life like one of my characters, which also involved living comfortably as a man, was abnormal and wrong for a 'girl'. So I confined my wishes to inside my mind and in my writing. My writing developed and progressed up until the time I came out: I existed in my own head as secretly male. I didn't know about being transgender then, I didn't know that I could legitimately want *to be* the opposite sex. I wanted to be a man in fantasy only; I dared not to dream that it could be reality. In reality I thought I was, and could only remain, a girl.

Writing religiously – poetry, short stories, anything – became a coping mechanism for me. When I was around thirteen, as a result of the difficulties I was experiencing at secondary school, I was diagnosed with depression by a counsellor after admitting self-harming and feeling very low. I think this was brought on by my mum's bipolar and depressive episodes, which I found hard to deal with, and I struggled to look after myself. Home life and bullying at school – although I tended not to show it – was wearing me down and I began to cut myself, sometimes even in school. No one knew apart from my best friend who was going through difficult issues herself. Through writing, I could express my anger and pain at the world. Although it wouldn't necessarily make my mind more at ease it gave me something to do, and people praised my writing online.

I kept a blog under the genderless pseudonyms 'Born in Hell', 'The-Engel' and 'Omega'. I don't have records of my writing nowadays as the site was shut down. Just a few poems, here and there, some old Word documents. Looking back on it now, I feel intrigued at how much I was exploring my feelings about sex, death and mortality. For onlookers, I imagine it was quite scary stuff.

As all of the characters I wrote about in my fiction were gay, or predominantly gay, you would have expected me to be a straight girl – most writers of these stories are. Not so! Although sexuality and gender identity aren't strictly related, I feel it's important to talk about my experiences with it as part of this book.

At secondary school I started exploring my sexuality. I identified both as bisexual and as a lesbian as I went through stages of liking both boys and girls and then just girls. I crushed hard on one of my female acquaintances for about a year; I was smitten by her, especially her beauty. I thought she was gorgeous. No one knew my secret until I confided in my best friend and I never told the girl in question. I was feeling more and more attracted to women as the years went by. Heidi Klum was the first woman I was *really* attracted to. I remember I had a *Guinness World Records* annual, and there is a picture of her in there looking fantastic in a sapphire-and-diamond-encrusted set of underwear and I would look at it constantly. This sparked off my coming out to my classmates in quite a dramatic way: a boy wanted to see this picture, so I cut the picture out of the book to show him. Inevitably, this got passed around the class, and so the rumours began that I liked looking at pictures of girls. As rumours about sexuality are, these were persistent and annoying, but I quickly found ways to deal with them. I laughed them off and said that I liked men as well, using the fact that I actually did to play down my attraction to women.

Often, I didn't know what to identify as and while I didn't explicitly confess I was lesbian I gave no comment on the accusations that I was. I was very pro-gay rights from an early age, and wasn't afraid to make that known. I never thought about gender at all; I had never heard about transgender people outside transvestites and drag queens.

I have no idea what people thought of my sexuality, as when I was identifying as bisexual I did have a boyfriend at school who had been a friend for some time previously. His name was Connor. We went out for about a year when we were thirteen or so, and were good friends before and after, but it wasn't very serious as we were only young and it fizzled out eventually. But even with that as 'common knowledge', people knew I liked girls, and with my outspoken, masculine and nerdy attitude, I was seen as a 'dyke'. Reactions were varied; I got comments of course, but nothing seriously nasty on account of my sexuality (a sickeningly common occurrence for LGBTQ teenagers is the vicious use of death threats). Plus I was never physically attacked.

My sexuality was fluid and changed on a regular basis. Some days I would be sure that I was lesbian and then the next day I would find men attractive and wonder why I thought I was lesbian in the first place. I had no problem identifying as either straight or lesbian, and it went in cycles. But after a while I decided that I liked men too much to be lesbian and I decided to accept my sexuality as fluid, which took me a while. I did like to be gay; I liked the 'feel' of it, the excitement. I knew I was queer, definitely, and I supposed 'lesbian' was the edgiest thing I could identify as. But I did like men no matter how I identified, and when I went through identifying as a lesbian, I had my 'exceptions', and I think many lesbians do. I never did have a proper girlfriend though!

Many trans men go through a 'lesbian phase', even if they end up being totally gay guys. I think that this is because when you identify as lesbian, it's OK to be more 'masculine', to be outspoken and feisty. That's how some lesbians are. So even if you don't fancy women 100 per cent, you feel safe within an area of non-normativity that *might* explain your personality and your feelings. And for me, this may explain why I fantasised about being a male character so much. I was very fluid in my sexuality and at points during my adolescence came out to my mum as both bisexual and lesbian. She accepted it. I knew she would as she has always been very open-minded and understanding, which I think is the reason that I don't remember having a 'coming out' as such. I just mentioned how I was feeling to her. There was never a big deal with my sexuality – it was what it was. I was proud to identify as 'lesbian' most times then: I was a *woman* who liked women. I was reaffirming my gender identity again, as well as giving two fingers to conformity. I knew though that I was a bad lesbian, and fancied guys a lot more than girls.

I felt no gender-related angst with my body during puberty at school until after I identified as trans when I was fifteen. I developed a disliking for my breasts and a longing to have male genitalia. I think this is the case for many trans people: it's only after they come out to themselves as male that they wish they looked more like one. However, there are those who have always felt some sense of discord with some parts of their body but didn't know why, or always hated them because they 'gave away' the fact that they were wrongly sexed. I was fine with periods and my boobs and, like many girls, wished I was prettier and that my hair was perfect and straight. Changing rooms were fine, although when I first came out as lesbian I got some comments from the other girls who I was changing with. These were mostly out of fear of me looking at them in a sexual way – but they soon died down. Actually, on the subject of gender stereotypes within sports at school, I was friendly with quite a cool group of girls, ones who were popular but didn't look down on me. They petitioned to be allowed to wear tracksuits instead of skirts and they all liked football or rugby and were very athletic. Somehow, I managed to get off any sporting activity for a long period of my time at school, which was great as I didn't enjoy exercise. This was usually due to faking illness or injury. Later on in the sixth form – when I had come out as male and when PE was still mandatory – my mum and I had a meeting with the head of my year who said that using the male changing rooms was out of the question and instead I would do work in the library.

So through secondary school and up until 2008, I identified as a weird gay woman who had crushes on guys. I was muddling through life. Then, everything changed.

Luisa: Holding on to threads

I first started feeling unwell in November 1994. I was thirty-one and Nat was just two years old. I can remember it clearly. I was outside in the back garden and, like a rush, all of a sudden I started shaking. I sat down on the patio step and felt very strange. At the time I remember thinking, 'What is happening to me? This is not me.' I felt as though I was standing out of myself, standing there beside myself, the self that was sitting down on the patio step. I felt anxious, panicky, my mind was racing and I just kept shaking. I was scared, very scared. After a while I calmed down, went indoors and never spoke of it. Over the next year I was up and down, sometimes full of energy and focused, other times tired and very emotional. I hid these feelings as best I could from those around me, putting on a mask of normality. I struggled on, then eventually went to see my GP for help. He put me on a low dose of antidepressants, which eventually stabilised my moods. I felt more even, calmer and energised.

A couple of years on and we were posted to Riyadh, Saudi Arabia. My marriage to my husband was already starting to give way at the seams; it had been slowly falling apart for the last couple of years. I was finding it increasingly difficult living with him. I didn't feel that we had a relationship based on mutual support and taking care of one another. I felt lonely in a loveless marriage that just seemed to be running on empty. There was no real or meaningful communication between us. We lived as strangers who were trapped within four walls and a domestic routine, nothing else. We both decided that we would continue with this posting as a family, but that we would have our separate bedrooms and we would both be there for Nat. It was very much a business arrangement with the reward of financial security at the end of our posting abroad. Initially I tried, I think we both did, but it's not possible to sustain any kind of a relationship if living with the other person feels so unbearable.

Nat, who was around six at this time, was picking up on the negative feelings. As adults we assume that we are hiding things well but children are a great deal more astute than we give them credit for. She was well aware that Mum and Dad were unhappy with each other. To the outside world we looked like a strong family unit, but in truth we were disintegrating by the day. It was a useless situation to be in for all of us.

To add to it all – I contracted chicken pox! There was an outbreak of it that year in Riyadh. Nat got it and as I never had it as a child, I got a very severe case of it. It was around 50°C in the shade so being quarantined indoors, even with the air-conditioning, was enough to drive anyone into a depression. Then, to add further to the difficulties, my pox became infected as a result of being anaemic. Quarantined, in a very unhappy marriage and with infected pox, I became extremely depressed. Once I was fit enough to travel I was medically evacuated back to London and spent a month at St Thomas's Hospital. The first two weeks were spent in their psychiatric ward. I knew I was suffering with mental health problems but after meeting some of the other patients I realised that I was not as unstable as I had first feared. I felt like an extra in the film *One Flew Over the Cuckoo's Nest*. I don't know how else to describe the sadness of life I saw there.

I made every effort to be on my best behaviour during my stay on the ward, making sure that I did and said all the right things so I could be discharged on to a *normal* ward. It was sad, unnerving and terrible. I felt let down, and I wasn't the only one on the psychiatric ward who felt this way. Where was the treatment plan, the counselling? Where was the proper due care and attention? The only care given was that of containment within the ward and handing out dosages of antidepressants and other mood-stabilising medication. If you asked to talk to a doctor, and were told that 'Yes, the doctor is due to see you tomorrow', tomorrow in fact could be the day after or the day after that. I felt uncared for and that my needs weren't being listened to.

After another two-week stay in a general ward I was discharged. All I wanted to do was get back to Riyadh and be with Nat again. I had missed her so much and had kept in contact by drawing funny cartoon pictures, which the welfare officer who visited me would fax over to Nat's dad in Riyadh. When I arrived back late at night, the first thing I did was go up to Nat's bedroom. She was fast asleep. I told her softly that Mama was back. She woke up sleepily and I will always remember the look of happiness on her face at seeing me. We gave each other a big cuddle (I just wanted to squeeze her really, really tight) and I sat on her bed in the half-light for a while. She went to sleep with a smile on her face that night. It was good to be back there for her.

I was still not well, though, and my depression soon returned. My posting was cut short due to my ill health and around 1999 I moved back to the UK and into the family home with Nat and my mother. I started divorce proceedings; we both knew that was the only solution forward and I had to embark upon a new beginning.

The millennium year came and went and I got through the next couple of years. I would be well for a while and then the depression would hit again. Emotionally I was up and down. I struggled, struggled and then struggled some more. My mother was a tremendous support, although she felt helpless in the face of my depression and could not understand why I suffered so much. Even though Mum could not understand what I was going through, she was always there. I am so grateful for her care and support, for looking after Nat during my deep dark days and for the unconditional love she gave me. She kept a daily routine going when without her there would have been none. I kept taking the antidepressants but there was little relief. It all culminated in another three-day spell in a psychiatric ward, again with the same usual standard of care I had been exposed to before: containment and drugs. It was three days too many to bear. I came out feeling just as ill as when I went in, only with a greater sense of guilt at having let Nat and my mum down by being so ill with depression. Depression is a wicked illness. It traps you in a dark isolated place where you are so wrapped up in your own pain that you shut out those around you. It is a selfish illness that strangles your capacity to communicate. Depression affects those around you, without you being fully aware of the hurt and distress that you are causing the ones you love. It is debilitating, leaving you at times holding on to a thread, second to second, minute to minute, willing the crippling darkness to somehow lift. Eventually, with further counselling and an increase in my medication, some normality was brought back into my life and to those I cared for.

I was now well enough to start work again and took a job as a civil servant in London. I felt focused once again and enjoyed the new challenges of my working life. My mental health stabilised. Then my mother died and my heart broke. The pain of this loss is one that I will never be able to put into words. How do you describe a feeling of wanting the whole world to stand still because you have lost part of your being? How can you make people understand the extent of your anger and pain when the force of it is incomprehensible? I confronted Mum's unexpected death by presenting an outward mask of strength and competence. Inwardly I was lost. Eventually I became worn down by the daily mental and physical battle of an outside normality I was trying to sustain and I crashed, inevitably, into a dark and terrible place again. There was a diagnosis of bipolar depression II, where your state of mind goes from very high to very low. It has taken a long time for me to return from this place but I have, and the relief really is beyond words. It makes me think of the famous saying that you can either get busy living or you can get busy dying. It has been so very hard but now with the right professional help, the right medication and the continued support from those who love and care for me, I can focus on the 'get busy living'.

An essential point of writing this chapter is to separate my mental health illness from the gender dysphoria of my son. The two are not inextricably connected. My son was born transgender, regardless of my mental health. I have met transgender people of all ages and from all walks of life, each of whom comes from a diverse and wide spectrum of social, cultural, ethnic and religious backgrounds. They were all born transgender regardless of this diversity. You do not choose gender dysphoria, it is already chosen for you. The simple fact is that Nat was always going to be Jon. This decision had already been made for him during my pregnancy. The choice he had was to accept and come to an understanding of what it meant to him to be transgender. He has chosen to live the life that he was meant to live and he has chosen to become the person that he was meant to be.

Three

Hard Times

Jon: Things get really bad

When I was fifteen, I spent a few months at the Bethlem psychiatric hospital in Beckenham, a twenty-minute drive from my home.

It had all started when I was thirteen and my grandmother had died, leaving my mum very depressed. Lala had been ill for a long time with heart problems and surgery had left her with complications – a stomach infection which became fatal. I remember going to see her in intensive care, with my then boyfriend. It was terrible and heart-breaking. Although we had had some falling-outs in my childhood due to the clash of our strong natures, and me being a typical teenager, she was the only one who was there for me when I needed her. She would cook nice food, wash my clothes, and generally be a second mum, with my dad only coming round to the house back then to pick me up for outings. I don't blame my father for not being around more; I preferred the quiet everyday setting with my grandma and I had a lot of contact with him anyway and liked seeing him for the fun times we had.

I remember the horror of intensive care. The wires, the bleeping and the screens with flashing lights. My mum, who had been there nearly every day to see Lala when she came out from surgery, warned me that it wasn't going to be a good experience. I steeled myself, but thought I would be able to cope. But when I went into the ward, the sight of the motionless bodies kept alive by pumps and drugs and tubes was too much for me to handle.

We reached my grandmother's bed at the end of the ward and I remember feeling a terrible jolt of shock. Her face, once rosy and tanned, was deathly pale; almost green. She looked thin, bony, withered. I instantly jumped behind my mother but she pushed me forwards and I locked my eyes with the pained ones of my grandmother, visible over the oxygen mask on her face. My mum told me to say hello and talk to her normally, as she had been doing. I couldn't. I could *not*. She didn't look like my grandmother to me, she looked like a corpse. I burst into tears, although my mum had said not to. I didn't want to speak to her and I didn't want to look at her. I wanted to run out of the ward and sit outside in the nice bright waiting room and play on my Game Boy. When my mum saw I wasn't going to be able to function, she let me go, and with relief I left after about five minutes.

That is my last memory of her. Lala died a few days later. I remember that it was a sunny day. I came downstairs and my dad was there. It must have been a school day, because I remember not expecting him. I looked at him, and at Mum, and immediately said, 'Is Lala dead?' And, of course, she was. I wasn't sad. I wasn't angry. I was relieved she was no longer suffering. My mum and dad hugged me, even though I didn't feel I needed one. And then I was offered an outing; I was happy at that and chose to go to the London Dungeons with my dad, while Mum had time to herself and made preparations for Lala's funeral. I remember having no particularly strong feelings about her death. I was sad at the loss, yes, but I felt more sadness for my mother, who had been closer to her than I had. It was clear that the loss of Lala had hit her the hardest.

After the death of my grandmother, when my mum found it increasingly hard to cope and look after me, I stayed at my dad's house during holiday periods with him and his new baby. Since my parents' divorce he had found a partner and lived in the East Midlands with her and their child. At first I enjoyed being around him and staying in his house – I got on well with his partner and her parents and during half-terms and summer holidays we spent the weeks travelling around north-east England to see his family. But as the baby grew that introduced stresses. On one occasion I begged Mum to come home – but I couldn't. Mum needed space to get better and I couldn't get the train down on my own. I remember locking myself in the bathroom when the baby's crying had made Dad short-tempered. The only solace I felt was hearing my mum's voice on the end of my phone I had brought in with me. I don't know how long I stayed in there but I knew that it was not the first time that I had wished myself away to my bedroom back at home. Mum was too ill to take me back so early and I did not want to ask my dad if he could take me back to London.

When things got really bad, when my mum started to get even more depressed and needed Dad to take care of me for a longer period, he was not contactable.

Towards the end of 2007, when I was fifteen, my mum's bipolar illness escalated. She was broken. She took a turn for the worse and was really very ill, not yet out of the grip of grief. I think I must have fed off her depression. It came to the point where we only left the house to get food from the local supermarket and, more often than not, Mum would order in a takeaway. I was constantly at the computer; I wasn't attending school; I wasn't taking care of myself. I was just listening to music and posting blogs, stories and poetry on the Internet. I had self-destructive thoughts and was morbidly fascinated with death, self-mutilation and pushing my body to the extreme. I was extremely skinny as a result of a lack of appetite and because there was little proper food in the house, just toast or snacks. I was a wreck, an unwashed, malnourished wreck. I think the depression just sucked us in, until it became a cycle that we couldn't break. Mum couldn't take care of me, Dad was not around and I couldn't take care of either of us.

Kathy, one of my mum's friends, came round and saw the sorry state we were in. I remember feeling angry at her for stating the obvious. 'Your mum isn't well,' she said. I knew that – we had been living like this for the past two months! I knew things were bad but I felt helpless to remedy our situation. It later became clear that Mum had asked several people for help before getting into this circle of depression. I discovered much later that when things got really bad my father was not there for me.

In early January, I tried to overdose on paracetamol. Looking back, I think it was more a cry for help than actually wanting to die. Somehow, the terrible situation I was living in had to end. It wasn't premeditated as such, I just had had enough. I remember being downstairs and raiding the cupboard for paracetamol – there wasn't much and I was too afraid to do something serious. Afterwards I went upstairs to tell Mum what I'd done, to shock her into action. I wanted to do something to instigate some sort of change. My mum called in the Bromley Mental Health team. When the medical professionals assessed the situation it was obvious that, for the time being at least, I couldn't be in that house any longer. I was a risk to myself and my mum couldn't look after me. The only option for me was to go into a mental health unit for adolescents, away from everything and to get help for my own problems.

Getting away from it all in the Bethlem hospital, I now realise, was a godsend. I went to the adolescent unit and was able to talk to other people face to face, have a stable routine and proper meals. After a week, Mum was allowed to come and visit me, but she was still receiving care at home and was too unwell to make it over. It would be another two weeks before she was well enough to come and see me. On her first visit we went for a walk through the Bethlem's extensive grounds, the first time we'd both been outside with each other for ages. We walked through the woods in the sunshine. It felt good to be doing something with my mum that was normal. On another occasion, my mum brought my cat to see me. I had called him Christmas, because I got him from a rescue centre just before one Christmas. I had always wanted a cat but we had never had one as my dad was not a pet person. Lala got him for me as a welcome home present when my parents returned from Saudi and got divorced. Mum brought him in his basket and he had a little red collar with a lead and I walked him round the garden at the front of the unit. I remember the other patients looking out of the windows. It must have been a surprising sight, no doubt about it. A cat on a lead being taken for a walk in the grounds of a mental hospital. Surreal but maybe quite apt!

Being around other people really helped me. Of course, there were bad times and my mental state got worse at a few points while I was inside, which was a period of about three months. However, I think this depression came from confronting my emotions. I eagerly awaited calls home, but at the beginning I felt depressed when I heard Mum was still doing badly. I tried not to think about this after a while and concentrated on getting better. At home when things were bad I was numb and subdued most of the time, and when I felt extreme emotions I couldn't really let go because Mum would notice if I did anything visibly extreme, like cry or kick off or punch things. I felt I could express myself more at the Bethlem as my behaviour wouldn't upset Mum and I had to get it out of my system. While I was never physically restrained, the panic alarm was set off for me a few times.

Although at times hard, my stay at Bethlem had a positive effect on me. The ward was nice and after a while I was allowed out for walks on my own to the nearby town to buy magazines and to look around the shops. There was a school attached to the ward which the patients attended and there were a variety of lessons: English, maths, science, IT, RE, PE, talks about personal hygiene and eating healthily and supervised trips out to parks and museums. I continued to do work for the GCSEs that I was taking that year – science, English and German. I adored the German language, and I received an A grade in my English coursework, but for the life of me I can't remember doing any science.

I was certainly not the 'worst' person at Bethlem; there were others who were more severely depressed or unstable than me. I was able to benefit from the group therapies and individual counselling, which really helped me. I also had something to work towards; I was planning to go to a Nightwish concert in March. They were my favourite metal band at the time and I knew I had to be stable by then for the doctors to feel secure enough with my progress to allow me to go up to London. I would be in Central London in a crowded space and could easily slip away if I wanted to. I was optimistic though as I was making good progress and showing reliability when I went out on my own. I didn't want to break the doctor's trust in me and have my independence taken away.

I liked my new routine and organised life and showing the new people admitted to the ward what it was like. I felt so much more protected, now that there were adults here who could care for me. Slowly I found optimism and strength from being at the Bethlem. I relearned social skills and how to cope on my own. I had a new respect for myself and had found the motivation to get on with life. This, along with my interest in schoolwork, being with people again and away from my stagnant depressed home life, contributed to the positive change within me.

I was out as lesbian at Bethlem and I was open and proud of this identity, which I'd become more secure in. (Even now I can never stay in the closet, being a proud queer.) During the time I was holed up at home I had begun flirting with girls on the Internet. I had an intense crush on one girl that I had met online. We had met on an art-sharing website and got chatting over comments. I introduced her to some bands I liked and we quickly bonded over our shared love of music. She lived in another time zone, so I talked to her every night for hours. I remember mentioning her to some people at the hospital and also crushed on two of the other girls there. One girl, who I discovered was bisexual, had a crush on me. Nothing came of it though: both of the girls I crushed on were straight and I wasn't interested in the girl who was interested in me. When I left hospital I remained friends with them and on one occasion we all met up in Camden, however I have had no contact with them in years.

Being a lesbian was an identity I carried on claiming up until the end of my hospital stay. I never thought about gender issues in the Bethlem; I still thought of myself as a lesbian/fluid female. I still did not know anything about being transgender at this point: I was still unaware of its existence. Besides, I had other issues that were on my mind – recovery from my depression and catching up on months of coursework and all the exam preparation that I had missed. My recovery, however, was slow, with lots of help and space away to think and recover from being stuck at home. I was starting to eat proper meals and put on weight again; I was thankful I felt healthy. It took a while, but I was ready to go back to school at the end of it, and was starting to attend lessons again on a part-time basis.

Coming to the end of my hospital stay, I felt well

again. In the last couple of weeks I spent there I felt secure and calm within myself and ready to get on with life. With my assessment for discharge coming up I felt sure that the doctors and staff would agree with this, and they did. Mum – who was much better now – was at this final assessment meeting along with the welfare officer for my school, my CAMHS (Children and Adolescent Mental Health Services) counsellor who had made the initial referral to the Bethlem, and the doctors and staff who had been responsible for my individual care. We all agreed that I had made significant progress, my mental and physical state had clearly improved and I was ready to be discharged. I would continue on medication and counselling support would be there if I needed it. I had a clear head now the fog of depression had lifted and coming into the summer refreshed and hopeful I was able to concentrate on my future.

Luisa: The pain inside

It had been a difficult year for my daughter and me. The recent death of my mother left me with a broken heart. Natasha did not talk about her grandmother and everything that reminded me of her I hid away. We had all lived together, three generations under the same roof, my mother, my daughter and me – I would often refer to us as 'the girls'. There was much love in our home and even though there were times when our three personalities would collide, it felt good being the three girls indoors. My mother had loved her granddaughter deeply.

I remember making a long-distance call to Nigeria when I was two months pregnant, as my mother was then still living with my father in West Africa. I told her that she was going to be a grandmother. At first there was no sound on the end of the line, then absolute joy in her voice as she repeated a couple of times that she just could not believe it. It would be her first grandchild. My mum was rarely speechless and her long silence had surprised me. A general Latino characteristic tends to be talking rapidly, and my mother tended to talk at double this speed! Speechless was definitely not in her vocabulary. She later told me that the news took her breath away. The next time this would happen was when I made another long-distance call to tell her that my scan showed that I would be having a girl.

Nat, now fifteen, had been very low for some time. School was an ongoing difficulty, not academically as she is a gifted student, but socially. She had always been on the fringes; it seemed to have started in her move from infants' to primary school and would continue until it became clear why. My daughter was a tomboy, happiest playing with the boys. At infants' school it was great, the boys and the girls all wore the same school uniform of tracksuits so Nat could rough and tumble to her heart's content. Whenever she had friends round, more often than not they were boys. She just clicked better with the boys and they clicked with her.

When she moved up to primary school things changed. Some of the girls were cruel and bitchy. As Nat was not your stereotypical girly girl she became marginalised, excluded from the girly circles. She was not accepted by them for being herself. She still played with the boys when they allowed her to, because now it was different and gender roles were being played out in the playground. There was no longer the acceptance of someone a little bit different from the others; that now became an issue.

There were times when I had to go into school and complain about the bullying. Looking back now I know that my daughter kept a great deal of pain inside and only when it became unbearable would she tell me of an instance of bullying. I imagine that she spent lonely times in the playground and that saddens me. Although she always seemed to be on the outskirts and continuously bullied, this did not stop her from being the individual that she needed to be. What she did have was tremendous resilience and a couple of boys that really were friends. The girls who accepted her being a tomboy were like my daughter, they too had a free spiritedness. They would be considered slightly quirky, different because like Nat they did not fit into a stereotypical box, whether this was in their choice of books, taste in clothes, music or the way they played. Nat got on best with children who refused to let boxes contain them. At the age of thirteen she took up medieval sword fighting. She was the only girl there, the rest were males. This was not a problem for the instructor or Nat; she was very good at sword fighting and they all accepted her. She was comfortable in this very individual choice and I always supported her in whatever she wanted to do. I was proud of her free spirit and courage to express her individuality and felt that this was important for her outlook on life.

Her move to secondary school was another step in our journey.

At this time both of us were struggling to cope. Nat was often very down, not wanting to go to school. When she did go she would return home withdrawn and unhappy more often than not. A day off school here and there eventually became months signed off with depression. Nat agreed to have counselling and was referred to CAMHS. She was lucky to have a very good counsellor who she was comfortable with. She slowly started to open up to him, but never mentioned any feelings or thoughts on gender during these sessions. Her sessions were private but on a couple of occasions (with Nat's consent) we would have a short time in her session together talking about her progress. She was prescribed anti-depressants and her mood seemed to stabilise a little, but she was still down. I also asked my GP for a referral for counselling to help me through my depressive state of mind. I struggled trying to keep a brave face on it all and maintain a front of normality. It all felt very bleak.

Four

Coming Out

Jon: I had to start somewhere

It was towards the middle of 2008 and I was home, much happier and free now to think a bit more about myself and my future. It was an odd moment, therefore, when I realised that I did not see myself as female any more. I was longing to be someone else but couldn't see myself as an older woman. Struggling to map out my future in my head, one day I took a Biro and a scrap of paper and tried to draw a picture of myself in several years' time. When I scribbled out my face, masking it with long hair to make it androgynous, I realised I needed a change. This time I didn't want to cover up who I felt I was, but to show it to the world.

I was lucky that I had a previous interest in queer issues from my days of questioning my sexuality. I had heard of the term 'genderqueer' (a term commonly used to describe a person with a gender outside male or female; it means not fitting into a neat male or female category, some people might identify as androdgynous, but this is not the only label under this category) before I went into hospital, and an echo of that resurfaced in my mind. Was this what I was feeling? I researched a name for my 'condition' and googled how I was feeling: a dissonance with my gender and a longing to be a man in the future. The term 'genderqueer' resurfaced and I read more about it in depth. I re-joined the Queer Youth Network where I had previously registered an account but never really logged in. This gave me an information database and connection with other young people, it gave me a link to my reality. In late 2007 I had joined QYN as a questioning lesbian, but now I realised that that label just didn't fit. At QYN, I had the opportunity to meet and talk to other young people who, like me, were questioning their gender and their options. These were the first people to accept and understand me. QYN was geared towards people aged thirteen to twenty-five, and I found there were lots of people around my age using the site. The online message boards were the only places where I felt I could be 'out' as trans.

There were meet-ups for London and the South-East, which were held monthly in Hyde Park. I went to my first meet-up in the summer of 2008. I cannot find the words to do justice to the people I met there. I can honestly say that if I hadn't found them, I would probably still be a desperately unhappy twenty-year-old. I met people my age who were unafraid of who they were and were living as openly LGBTQ and proud. I was instantly taken at how confident they were and how much fun they had as a close-knit group. They were very respectful to all manners of gender identity and presentation – along with introducing people by name we were also asked to say our preferred pronoun (such as he, she, they, etc.). I met genderqueer people there that day, the first face-to-face meeting with genderqueer people I ever had. In the park was an old large tree that we called 'our tree'. It was our meeting point and was like a hollow pudding. Its leaves and branches bent over and touched the ground in a dome shape and you could enter into its tent-like canopy and climb onto the sturdy outer branches. I remember having a conversation on the top of 'our tree' about how I felt and identified. I had introduced myself there to people as 'either Natasha or Jon', being unsure of my identity at the time and still nervous about introducing myself as male. But as the day wore on

I became more and more comfortable with people using my male name and referring to me by the male pronoun. I was simply having fun in a safe space, with my gender being fully accepted. As I spent more days as Jon, I grew in confidence that this was something I could take outside of this group: I could actually see myself living my life this way.

We didn't solely talk about gender and sexuality but about everything. I added some people on Facebook and actually had a social life for the first time in a long time. I went to a Slayer gig with someone I had met there and I was invited to house parties after the monthly meets. We also went to London and Brighton Pride together, which was a euphoric experience for me. I had never travelled outside of London on my own before and going to Brighton, although it is a relatively short train journey from Waterloo Station, felt like a huge milestone. Back in 2008, the Brighton Pride march was much more 'open' than the London march. Anyone could come off the streets and join in the parade, whereas that isn't really possible in the capital. It is less heavily policed in Brighton and there are fewer protesters. At Brighton Pride I only saw about two protesters, whereas at my first London Pride a gaggle of around fifteen stood many metres back from the march in a fenced-off enclosure. They were guarded like sheep in a pen by a row of policemen who stood silently as we challenged them and they held and waved their banners with messages from the Bible and shouted damnation and hell-fire back at us for the sins we had brought upon ourselves. In Brighton it was raining on the day of the march, and being on the coast it just pelted down. Singing and marching in the rain is an amazing experience – calling out for diversity and equality, young people clambering over the barriers to join us, and many joining in the singing on the side-lines. There was a real feeling that we were the new proud and queer generation, and we would fight for this equality and diversity. The block I was marching with started out as a few people carrying a few homemade banners. Towards the end of the parade, our block was a sea of glitter and rainbow-coloured bodies: around a hundred people had jumped out of the crowd to join us. Although that was the only time I went to Brighton Pride, I have been to every London Pride since, but that amazing experience will always be the first and best for me.

It was around this time that I spoke to my mum about being 'genderqueer'. I mentioned it to her one evening out of the blue, testing how she felt about gender. I explained the term and said that I may iden-tify with it. She accepted what I told her – no big freak out. She probably didn't understand its meaning but just accepted that I was exploring my identity as a person. I didn't feel particularly nervous telling her about my genderqueer identity; I suppose at that time I didn't know how much I was going to go through, or even if I wanted to start a male transition.

And still, even though I didn't identify as male or female, I felt much more comfortable presenting as a male, and being thought of as one, and I presented myself as male at QYN from then on. At the next meet I went to, I didn't introduce myself with an 'or' between my male and female names – from now on, at QYN I was 'Jon'.

Jon is not as exciting a name as some choose; some trans guys pick exotic, elaborate names. There's no special reasoning behind me choosing my name as there is for some trans people. Some ask their parents what they would have been called if they have been assigned their proper gender at birth and take that name, some choose a name of someone who they admire or strongly identify with. I, however, have no Jons in my life. I do not know where my chosen middle name 'Andrew' comes from, it just hit me as a fitting middle name and I liked the sound of it. There was a boy in my year at school called Andrew, and when I mentioned to him that I had chosen Andrew as my middle name he looked very confused.

As living socially as male within my queer friendship group became my norm, there became little doubt in my mind that I wanted to transition medically. During the beginning of that summer I was dressing in more typically masculine clothes every day. I had an article of clothing called a binder, with which I flattened my breasts, and usually wore band tees and cargo trousers for going out. I was using my male name and pronoun with the friends who knew about my decision, and choosing the male toilets whenever I needed to use the bathroom.

It was only at home that I was 'in the closet'. I still hadn't told my mum and from the outside I just looked like a kinda butch girl. But the person I could see in my future didn't look like this, not by a long shot. The person in my future, I began to realise, had a deep voice, facial hair and he was definitely a man. I knew I couldn't possibly start my medical transition without my mum's help. Throughout my life she had been my rock, always loving, always accepting, and I knew she was aware about my fluid sexuality. She knew about my circle of LGBTQ friends but as far as Mum was concerned she was accompanying me to these groups because of my sexuality. I started to drop hints to her about presenting or wanting to present as male. Hints, for example, about what name I was using with friends. Her understanding was that I was still exploring my sexuality, nothing else.

I distinctly remember the day when Mum and I were on my way home from my very first meet-up with PACE, a mental health and well-being group for young LGBTQ people. I'd found PACE by searching for more LGBTQ groups for young people in London. The meet-up with PACE had taken place in the middle of Soho Square. Mum had come along to accompany me and meet with the youth workers and other parents. It was packed with young people from the three youth groups PACE ran. I never really got to know anybody there that well, even though I did end up doing volunteering for the organisation in 2010. I found QYN more to my liking, and I found it easier to build friends there: it was a much more informal setting, and seemed more like a group of friends than a structured youth group.

Some of us quieter and shy people sat in a circle and had a good time, whereas all the other queers talked and messed around like they had known each other for years. They probably had. It was a good meet-up and I left feeling quietly happy that I had made some new friends that day, something I had been practising doing since leaving the Bethlem. That and actually having a social life outside of school for the first time.

During the meet I left a trail of rather large (I thought) breadcrumbs and hoped Mum would follow them and ask me outright why I was dressing in boys' clothes and if I wanted to be a boy. I was always waking up with the feeling of living a double life in those days, but not caring if my masculinity was visible. I remember not really wanting to come out to my mum, but knowing that I had to. This was serious, and I was serious about wanting and needing to transition. I was just too scared to express it with words, to have 'the talk'. Looking back now, there was no reason to fear. But, among the stories that had given me hope, I had also heard too many devastating stories about not being accepted and I wanted to have my mother in my future.

On the way back home, I received a text from one of the members I'd met there, asking whether they should call me my female name or 'Jon' from then on. I'd introduced myself as female, but only as I was leaving did I give this person the option of using my male name. I replied and Mum asked me who I was texting. I said, nervously: 'Oh, they're just wondering whether they should call me Nat or call me Jon.' And I left it at that. Mum didn't say anything and I didn't push the subject. She has a habit of not showing any extreme reactions to news one way or the other. I still don't know if I like the fact that she's calm despite whatever news I tell her or if I need more of a reaction. That was the last time we spoke about anything relating to gender, until the night I officially came out to her two months later.

The evening I came out to Mum I was on the Internet on the QYN forums. I was in turmoil. I knew the time had come to tell Mum. I needed to help her to understand me. But of course, I was shit scared. Coming out as trans can be, and often is, far more difficult than coming out as lesbian, bi or gay. For one thing, there are more commonly held misconceptions about trans identities than there are about gay or lesbian identities. There are more taboos, it's less known and not spoken about as much. I later found out that prior to me coming out to her as trans and educating her about it, Mum had only heard of drag queens, transvestites and the media presentation of trans women and didn't know anything more about it. She'd just never had to think about these issues and had only seen the media portrayal of trans people. Trans people were the subject of sensationalised news stories, or fleetingly mentioned in articles about gay rights or were the divas in gay night clubs. They weren't everyday people. Now, my mum is well clued up on trans issues and remains open-minded, but I can't imagine what must have been going through her mind when she found out her only child was one.

And there's more involved in coming out as trans than there is as coming out as gay or lesbian. For many people, being trans is a process that will last a lifetime. For many, it's a journey of financial difficulty, physical pain, medical treatment, depression and legal recognition for the rest of your life. Striving constantly to be fully recognised as a person, striving to have a little M or a little F on official documents, striving for those people who shout abuse at you in the street to learn about what's involved. And for many people who live outside the binary of male and female, it's a struggle to live in a culture where you do not legally exist.

But I knew I had to start somewhere – even at fifteen I knew that this journey was right for me. That night was to be my true setting off point.

I don't remember what day it was, or even now what month it was in 2008 that I came out to my mum. I remember it was the evening. My mum was downstairs on the sofa watching TV. I finished my blog, which I had kept since joining QYN, switched off my computer, gritted my teeth and walked downstairs. This would be my first real 'coming out' session about my transgender identity. At school, I was slowly starting to present as male and had asked some close friends (my best friend and another gay guy I trusted) to use 'Jon' and 'he'. But they did it in bewilderment and I didn't like to press the matter of my gender at school. I was still an odd bisexual lesbian to them, who was starting to cut her hair shorter and shorter. But this moment was the first big step. Hovering by the radiator opposite the living room, I was stuck for words. How do you even begin a conversation like this? And where from? There are many different ways trans people out themselves to family and friends – some may choose to write a letter or an email or talk over the phone. The only way that I was comfortable with doing it was face to face. I thought this was a good way of coming out to someone, as they have the chance to ask questions, you have the chance to answer, and nothing gets drawn out too much.

Looking up from the TV, Mum saw I was dithering and asked what was wrong. I remained silent – my mind blank. Now I was down here I couldn't just go back upstairs, it would look strange. I'd already set my mind to it. I mumbled 'Nothing . . .' but still I didn't budge. Would I just blurt it out or sit down and have a clear, succinct talk about it? For moments more I just stayed put, glued to the radiator, willing that she would guess and do the hard work for me. I still dithered, until she asked: 'Is it something to do with your body?' That wasn't quite it, but it was still something I could clutch on to as words were failing me. I replied that it was. She asked what in particular about my body I was upset about.

For the life of me, I still don't know why I said what I said. It wasn't completely true, it sounded stupid and I still cringe whenever I recall it. But explaining my situation 'clearly and succinctly' was not something I could do at that moment, so I suppose it was probably the best I could have come up with. I said, 'My boobs.' My mum asked what was wrong with them. I said that I didn't want them; and then I came out in a rush and garbled, 'I want to be a boy.'

The catharsis of coming out to my mum was immense, and I cried from relief. We hugged and I cried for a long time after that. We spoke for over an hour. Her reaction, of course, was more than I had expected. With something like this what reaction can you truly predict? Like everything else I had told her about myself, she accepted it, even if she did not fully understand it. She said she loved me no matter what and that was all that mattered. And in a parent–child relationship that is all that should matter, whether or not a parent agrees with what the child has revealed to them.

After we'd spoken, I left to post a blog on QYN about it. I don't know what must have been going through her head. I'm just thankful she's had the strength (at least in front of me) to keep calm and carry on. The responses I got online were ecstatic and supportive, and there was a kind of 'welcome to the team' vibe, as one member linked me to the binding thread on the trans youth board and told me to 'get started' on my transition.

And that was it: the official start of my life as 'myself'. The end of the beginning.

Luisa: A time for loss

Eventually, Nat was well enough to go back to school but the unhappiness continued. She went from having a day that was OK to not eating and spending hours on the computer. Trying to talk about the situation was difficult for us both. Talking to friends who also had teenagers gave me some false reassurance that it was just the growing-up thing, a teenage thing, hormones. I felt thankful that some of the stories I was told by parents were not mine, the arguments, door slamming, demands, sexual exploits, to name but a few from a long list that some of these exasperated parents had to deal with. I would soon learn that even though I hadn't had to deal with the majority of these scenarios with my daughter, those same parents would also be thankful that my story was not theirs.

I cannot remember the date or even which particular day of the week it was when my daughter eventually told me her 'secret'. I know it was midweek. I was tired from work, I had come in and gone through a usual domestic routine: put the washing up away, loaded the washing machine, fed the cats, fed the goldfish and finally fed Nat and me. Sometimes she would eat upstairs while on the computer. I would try and dispel my feelings of poor parenting by telling myself that at least that way she would maybe eat a bit more than usual by being distracted online, rather than sitting at the table taking two mouthfuls and saying she was not hungry any more. So she was on the computer again and I was downstairs watching something or other on the TV. Something pretty meaningless, I was definitely too tired to concentrate much.

It was getting late so I stood at the bottom of the stairs and called up to my daughter loud and clear that it was time to switch off and get to bed. We would now go through the well-rehearsed computer lockdown scene. It goes something like this:

'Nat you have forty-five minutes'.

Response was usually a grunty 'OK.'

About thirty minutes later. Bottom of stairs again. 'You have fifteen minutes.'

Response a pissed off 'Yes, Yes.'

Roughly fifteen minutes later. Bottom of stairs. 'Right, time to switch off and bed, it's school tomorrow'.

Response varies, from a surly 'OK' to a teenage 'Yeah, yeah, OK, I heard you the first time' to a loud curt *'I know!'*

I imagined all of these would be accompanied by a particular gesture that seems to be hardwired into the hormonal brain of all teens. It is the eye-rolling-silent-whatever gesture. This gesture seems to be pretty much universal and can be embellished with a few variations such as a loud heavy sigh or a combination of hand gestures.

I went back to the sofa and watched TV again. I could hear Nat upstairs, walking backwards and forwards between my room and hers; she was definitely not getting ready for bed. I just left it, thinking that I was too tired to battle with her. Ten minutes later she was still pacing around upstairs. Then I heard her coming downstairs and walk into the living room.

She stood and leaned against the radiator. She looked very tired. She was still in her school uniform, bags under her eyes and a strange look on her face. She looked so vulnerable and pale standing there. I just wanted her to get into bed, it was late and we were both tired. She just stood there. I could sense that something wasn't right. I asked her what was wrong and she mumbled 'Nothing . . .' and carried on just standing by the radiator.

I asked her to come and sit down next to me and tell me what was wrong. She came over and sat down on the other sofa. I asked again what was wrong. No response, she just looked pained and uncomfortable, arms folded and slightly hunched over. She then said she had to tell me something. Inside I had this moment of panic. Even through our difficulties our bond was always there. What was she going to tell me that I didn't know already? I remember thinking 'Oh God, don't be pregnant' and 'Please don't tell me you're on drugs.' I couldn't think what else it could possibly be. She mumbled something about her body. I said, 'What is wrong with your body?'

'It's my boobs.'

'What's wrong with them?'

'I don't want them.'

Then she said that she felt like a boy and started crying.

I could not comprehend what my child had just told me but my first instinct was to leap over to her on the other sofa and hold her in my arms in a protective hug. I wanted to comfort her and try to ease her pain while she cried. I remember saying that we will deal with this. Looking back now I remember a feeling that I had at the death of my mother. You are suspended in a numb place, confused and lost. I did not cry that night.

I checked on her during the night, she had gone to sleep at last. I, on the other hand, had little sleep, thoughts pounding around in my head, not able to take in the meaning of the previous hours. I remember waking up the next morning and for a moment not registering the events of the night before. My usual morning thought process started: time to get Nat up for school, make her packed lunch, feed the cats, do this, do that. Then I remembered her words, all this in a second of waking. I overwhelmingly felt that suspended and strange place again.

That morning was the start of our journey.

Five

Coming Out Again

Jon: Why I'm not stealth

If you're a non-straight person, the chances are that you're always going to be coming out. Even if you don't overtly 'come out', you still might mention that you have a same-gender partner, or use male or female pronouns for an ex, which means you've outed yourself anyway. Any accidental slip of the tongue and you're out. Every time you meet a new person in your life, be it new friends, family you've not seen for a while, bosses and co-workers, you'll inadvertently come out simply by mentioning mundane facts about yourself. Of course, you might keep your sexuality quiet, if you really want to, but generally, every non-straight person 'comes out' at least once in their life.

The process is even harder when you are transgender. In the early stages of social transition, avoiding coming out to anyone is nigh impossible: you've got to tell someone, a parent, a friend or a teacher, that you'll be changing things about yourself, such as your pronoun or name. You can't *not* come out, especially if they become curious and ask you about your behaviour, such as binding your chest, wearing very different clothing or why your friend referred to you as a girl or a boy – the little things, the hints that may give your shift in gender identity away. Trans people usually don't have a choice: if you want to be known as something different from what people have known you as for years, you've got to tell them.

There's always the option to move somewhere different, and start afresh as your affirmed gender. But for many trans people, especially younger trans people, moving somewhere you're not known simply isn't an option, although it may become one later in life. Being 'different people' in different situations is often a reality – for example, with my early transition to my queer friends, I was Jon, a guy, but at school I was still perceived as female, and only slowly starting to come out. For many people, they may be out socially, but professionally in the closet, as they may feel awkward or scared about transitioning at work, or even applying for work as their gender if they don't look 'convincing enough', fearful of discrimination and victimisation.

A trans person is going to be coming out more than a person of a non-normative sexuality would. Mistakes about pronouns, not passing as your gender and having to correct people, informing sexual partners, informing friends, new and old, are just some of the times when people may need to be corrected. If you do end up growing close to someone, you need to inform them before they have a chance to find out your past for themselves, if they see you as a cis person, due to the fear of being outed accidentally one way or another. Often, being outed accidentally happens through social-networking sites: scores of trans friends, old photos, trans events you're attending, can make the other person think something is up. It does feel that a trans person spends their life revealing their gender identity to everyone, a never-ending circle of trepidation about a person's reaction and the looming fear that they will find out anyway through other people even if you don't want them to. The frustration and pain of not passing, and forcing yourself to be outed is a common occurrence. A 'sir' there or a 'madam' here, or a shop assistant not allowing you to use the changing room of your choice and again it's out with the gender.

Often, our gender identity is dragged out of us

against our will in these situations, and having to go through the whole spiel once again is very disheartening. Either that, or you let everything pass with a dismal acceptance that you will never ever be seen as the gender you are. The early days of transition for many are the worst days and this endless coming out, for some, is still an occurrence years down the line into their transition. For some living a genderless presentation, coming out is as simple as walking down the road and people's heads turning.

Many trans people don't like to come out to everyone. Many trans people don't have the answers to all the questions; some are still trying to work it all out themselves. It can be tiring being constantly asked if you are a he or a she. You get tired of trying to explain that it isn't a choice, you were just born with something called gender dysphoria, and for the love of God no, you haven't had 'the op' yet.

A fresh start suddenly sounds awesome. Going 'stealth', as trans people call it, sounds brilliant. You live solely and full-time as your affirmed gender, relying on your ability to pass 100 per cent. You don't disclose your trans status, or your past life, to anyone. You are who you are. This may mean making several different Facebook accounts, one for new friends and colleagues, one for your 'trans friends' and 'other life'. A double life once again, but this time very different

– and for many, so much better. For others, stealth may mean not identifying with the trans community any more. You may finish transition or finish exploring your gender identity, whether that means finishing or beginning medical procedures, and then move on. No more word about it, like it was a problem that you've dealt with that now plays no part in your life. For many, this is a valid way of looking at being trans.

I don't look at it that way. I will never be stealth. I can't. I've done a documentary, I've written this book and I'm out in general. Even now, always passing 100 per cent, there is no question about what I identify as. A person could hear about me as some guy from a documentary, and then once again I'm out.

It was something that I had to think about very carefully when I was first deciding whether to take part in the documentary: what if I wanted to be left alone in later life, what if I wanted to be one of those people who want to leave their trans status behind them? I was still young, the documentary would out me in a very broad and public way, and then what could happen? Though these doubts played on my mind, I didn't really stress about it. I was only just starting to pass 100 per cent, and answering questions and correcting people about my gender identity seemed to be the norm. I could handle a bit more of that. I didn't want to dwell on the other consequences of what being out could entail. If I dwelt on the fact that a person might possibly attack me if they found out I was a 'tranny', it would be unproductive. If everyone kept in the closet because of their fear of being hated, nothing would ever change. I believe that openly trans people have to be visible. People's knowledge, ignorance and fear *need* to be challenged by education. Maybe – hopefully – this will lead to a day where everyone is educated by everyone else about trans issues, and it's not just left to individual members of the trans community. I also believe there is such a vital need for trans people who aren't afraid to say that they are trans to be role models for other trans people, and that differences in gender and gender identity are positive and beautiful and *normal*. If everyone lived as stealth all the time, there wouldn't be a supportive and vibrant trans community, maybe not even a trans community at all. And a trans community, or trans safe space, is vital for continuing trans struggles and for mutual support, especially for younger people.

I want to be one of the people who aren't afraid to educate and answer questions. This is a large part of why I need to live as openly trans and I believe I will identify as transgender for the rest of my life. I am proud of who I am and I don't need to hide this. I don't always choose to come out to people, and as a result of my medical transition people don't question my gender. But there are many situations where I do like to talk about it, and take the opportunity to be as open as I can about it. And if there was anywhere I felt I couldn't be open about it, regardless of whether I chose to come out or was outed, I wouldn't like that situation. My journey and experiences as a young trans person is something I hold dear to me. The inspirational people I've met, the many things I've learned; I want to pass on those experiences to others. I want to be visible as a trans person in my everyday life. You need to have more than a little pride when so many people don't understand you and you are having to deal with adversity, at times on a daily basis.

Many people love being stealth, for comfort and to just live hassle free and unburdened by people knowing they're trans (which could ultimately lead to people's perceptions being coloured, even if you can pass 100 per cent). But for me, it wouldn't work. And I'm OK with that.

Coming out to yourself

As I mentioned before, coming out takes place in various situations and to various people. But before everything, and most importantly, the first person I came out to was myself. Everyone needs to come out to themselves; it's the first step to self-acceptance of an identity. You need to accept yourself before you can move on.

Accepting yourself as trans can be difficult as there's more baggage associated with being trans than there is with sexuality. It doesn't just involve how you define your sexuality; your gender and your gender presentation permeates into every aspect of your life, affects how the world relates to you and how you relate to the world. And not only are you seen, and going to be seen, differently, but you're going to run into hate because of it. I suppose that's one thing accepting yourself as trans and accepting yourself as non-straight have in common: if you choose to be open about this, you're bound to run into some sort of trouble. But where a queer person's sexuality may not manifest itself in any outward signs, a trans person's identity *needs* to come out; it needs to be shown, and it needs to be lived in order for the person to move on with their life. Depression, anger, self-loathing and self-esteem problems, self-harm – all of these can be a result of trying to lock up a gender identity that is longing to come out. Self-destructive feelings and behaviours can be the result of waking up and once again facing the difficult realisation that you're eons away from achieving the first steps of living as a gender billions of people take for granted.

Frustrations that hamper a trans person may

not affect a cis-gendered queer person. For a trans person, you are reminded of your birth gender every day as your body is a constant reminder of it (and for many female-bodied people, a certain monthly reminder is inevitable). When I had just identified as bisexual and then as a lesbian, I was only aware of my sexuality when I saw an attractive person or read something online that I identified with. When you are stuck inside a body that you detest, and you feel the utter sense of detachment that comes from that (the 'dysphoria' in 'gender dysphoria'), then being trans is hard, and it's something that you don't want to be. It's hard that some people see you (and will always see you) as a freak because you were born in the wrong body. You might feel jealous that they, the lucky ones, don't have to think about it at all whereas you have to re-start your life *again*. You will never be treated the same as a 'normal man' or a 'normal woman'. You will be for ever a second-class citizen, portrayed as a cross-dressing fetishist by the worst of the media. And perhaps you also experience an inner transphobia – that you believe all of the bad things people say about 'trannies'. *They* can't be you, surely? You can't accept this. You don't want to accept this.

For many trans people self-acceptance takes a long time, especially when there are no points of support or role models whom you can look to for guidance. Self-acceptance as trans is also a lot harder when you don't fit the trans stereotypes. If you're not a masculine-enough trans guy or a feminine-enough trans woman you may think that you're lying to yourself and that you shouldn't be trans.

I've always been comfortable with accepting my gender identity in its many forms, I just let myself go with it. Rolling with it seems to be my default outlook on life. I'm still not sure if it's the best one. I tend to 'go with the flow' with a lot of things and often wonder if I should get wound up about things more. Sure, there have been days when it was very hard for me to cope with the harassment and the gender dysphoria, but I never shied away from my trans status. I may have wished things were different, but I knew who I was and I couldn't change those feelings. I never tried to pretend it didn't exist and I didn't want to bury it. Maybe that was because from fairly early on I always had a place to ask questions and people who I could talk to. I didn't keep my feelings to myself, and I inte-grated myself fully into the London trans community. Meeting other trans people led to the realisation that there were people who were living with this, and they were happy and proud, and accepted themselves. I think if I hadn't had this, I really wouldn't know how to deal with anything.

You cannot change being trans, but you can change how you view it and how you deal with it.

Coming out to family

For many trans people, coming out to family is a completely disheartening experience. I know people who have been disowned outright and people who have been blamed and victimised by their own families for daring to tell them how they truly felt. I am lucky to have had a relatively perfect coming-out experience regarding my own family.

Of course, my mum is the most accepting, even though she must be the one who finds it hardest to deal with. To let go of the past, to see the person you gave birth to change completely and to witness the physical process of transitioning into male taking hold, erasing the familiar face of your daughter. I know it's been difficult for Mum to understand my feelings, even though she's always accepted me for who I am and loved me. She's just always been there, and always been open to talk through things with me, and go to trans events to learn more. Her willingness to be a part of my life and to understand me is a blessing, and I am very grateful for her. We recently spoke together about my childhood, and how she wants to make a scrapbook for me. She said before, she wanted to make a scrapbook of 'Natasha', but now, she realises that this would be redundant for me. We're now going to make a scrapbook of *my* childhood, for both of us. We're going to choose the pictures together, be they of me in a dress or playing with a male friend. I know this is a big step for her – to come to terms that my childhood wasn't 'Natasha's' childhood. She can't refer to me as Jon when talking about the past, but this is OK. She's done so much already with adapting to my transition, and besides I can't begin to understand her emotions fully. But we both love and respect each other, and we try to understand each other's feelings and, as cheesy as it sounds, that's all that needs to happen.

My father, on the other hand, has not been there for me during transition. I haven't spoken to him properly since I stayed with him when Mum was ill in 2007 and he eventually stopped contacting us. Before the documentary came out we told him about my transitioning to male, and that he had a son now. I don't feel he cared enough about me, about us as a relationship – he sent me a letter, saying that he accepted it and my next birthday and Christmas cards were in my new name. Since he moved away with his new family, I've felt that there hasn't been any meaningful expression of love from him. I got no sense of love from the letters and cards I had from him.

I wonder if at twenty, and a few years past being a

legal adult, I am now completely out of his life. I think my mum is more hurt at the lack of contact with me than I am. She's angry with him for not being there as a father should be. And yes, I feel that he's done that and I am saddened.

His family, on the other hand, are wonderful. My aunts and uncles are accepting and loving, even his partner's parents never failed to send me vouchers and birthday and Christmas cards, which I'm always surprised and pleased to receive! My mum called one of my aunties, and her reaction to my transition can be seen on the documentary – it was an amazing and brilliant moment, and we are still in contact.

My dad's mum took longer to accept me. She admitted she found it hard to think of me as Jon, and as her grandson, but she still loved me, and never fails to write or send me Christmas and birthday presents. She addressed the cards to her lovely 'grandbairn', which is a gender-neutral way of saying grandchild. But I got a surprise one Christmas when she put 'Jonathan' inside the card. I'm not sure whether it would be too much of a shock for her to see me again – I look so obviously nothing like the girl who she last saw years and years ago, nothing like a 'bairn' at all.

The reaction from my Spanish family has been the biggest surprise of them all. They're all Catholic, so my mum and I had no idea what their reaction would be. Before I saw them after I had transitioned I hadn't seen them since I was fourteen so it was quite nerve-racking. But they were brilliant – one of my cousins told the rest of the family face to face about me transitioning and they accepted everything.

Coming out to friends and school

School. Well, this is where most of my coming outs took place, and where my transformation from socially female to socially male took place most visibly. When I entered Year 11 in September 2008, after some of my GCSE exams in the summer, I was still in female uniform and I still had my female name on the register. After I had come out to my mum, I knew that I wanted to transition at school. In the autumn, I had started to ask some of my friends who I trusted to call me 'Jon' and use male pronouns, even though I was still presenting as female (and as far as I can remember, I was still wearing a skirt!). I began to explain to them who I was; that I was questioning my gender identity and that I was a boy, even though I was still figuring it out for myself at the time. I can't say I lost any friends at all, and many were fantastic about it, even if they didn't really understand who or what I was, or why I was changing my name and pronoun. A few of them were blasé, but many of them tried, at least, to remember, and corrected themselves if they messed up. A few other people who weren't my closest friends knew, too. They'd heard it along the grapevine, or I'd started to get more confident in asking the other students to refer to me as male, and they were fine with that – my form group, with the exception of a few who found it hard to deal with, were especially accepting, and even commented to the form teacher that I was going by 'Jon' now (the poor teacher had no clue about this).

Lisa, one of my best friends – who has been my best friend since the beginning of secondary school – has stuck by me all the way. Even though I left the sixth form early, and we haven't been in touch as much as I'd like since, I still regard her as one of the most amazing and accepting people I've come across. We first met in Year 7. We had so much in common, and she was a genuinely nice person. We grew up together, and explored the same sorts of issues together: general teenage angst, emotional and relationship troubles, which further escalated for me when my mum was having trouble with bipolar depression and I was locked in my room with only my bad teenage poetry and a fantasy world of made-up characters. She read those bad pieces of poetry and she enjoyed my creative side, even though it often scared me to think that I was being sucked into a world of my creation, that often I was escaping too far from reality.

Naturally, as a result of this understanding and closeness, I developed a crush on her at one point. But that didn't materialise into anything and we remained tight friends. Inseparable. She was one of the few people with whom I truly felt comfortable and could talk to her about anything. When I came out to her as bisexual, she didn't make a big deal out of it; she just saw me as a person who she loved.

We were very close friends, but we weren't carbon copies of one another (although I have to admit, I did influence her music taste!). We just got one another on a level beyond fashion sense or music taste. I can't remember if coming out to her as trans was anything momentous, it probably wasn't. She would have been accepting and caring and she would have just taken it in her stride, like all of the other things I've ever told her about me. I think with most of my friends it was more of a gradual process of coming out: hinting, reminding them of my name, referring to me as a guy. Writing this, I realised that I've never thanked her for being my best friend throughout my difficult secondary school life, for trying to understand my depression and the trouble with my mum, for being with me during the turbulence of my identity, and for trying the hardest to remember my male name and to accept me as a guy. Thinking about this as I wrote, I messaged her on Facebook, telling her how much her friendship has meant, and still means to me today. She replied to me: 'You know what, Jon, I love you for the crazy person that you are and our memories, and not for your gender. With that in mind, you make a really fit boy!'

After my mum and I talked a lot we decided that if I wanted to I could transition starting as male in January 2009, which would give me a few months of living and presenting as male at school before going into the sixth form. Mum initially had thought it would be best for me to wait until I was already in the sixth form or college to start transition. She knew that it would be hard for others to adapt to this change, and was naturally scared of the abuse and victimisation I might face. But I knew that I had to get everything started now, so that I could be comfortable with presenting as male when I started wherever I would go to in September (which would happen to be the sixth form of the same school). Before the Christmas break, I legally changed my name by deed poll to Mr Jonathan Andrew Edwards, so I could then get my name changed on my school documents and other documentation. I still occasionally get letters addressed to Natasha, and it makes me smile to know that I probably don't need to open that letter as it has no relevance to Jon. I came into school with the deed all stamped, and the head of my form signed it off. It was set. Mum and I had a meeting with the headmistress. She had agreed that I could start transitioning at school and staff would be made aware of this. She made it clear to us that they would take any bullying or abuse seriously and that I was to report it if it happened. And I always did. Since coming out of hospital my confidence in dealing with situations and asking for help was sky high.

Toilets were an issue though. I really didn't want to use the boys' toilets as I knew what many of the boys at my school were like, and I knew that they were going to be the ones to give me the most trouble. I didn't want to face the chance of getting abuse every time I went to the toilet, but nor did I want to use the female toilets. After some discussion the best option seemed to be to activate my school card so I could open the accessible toilets and use them instead, which I was pleased about. Even when I moved up to the sixth form a year later, I still didn't use the male toilets, but preferred to use the staff or accessible ones, one time much to the confusion of one new staff member who hadn't been told that I was trans! Some of my friends who have transitioned at school, or are in the process of transitioning there, use their gender toilets rather than an accessible one and hold their head up high. I just made things easier for myself; I didn't want any more trouble than I knew I would get.

I don't think I underestimated the severity of the

abuse I would get in January, as well as during Year 11, but I think I did underestimate just how relentless people were going to be. My transition at school was my first exposure to transphobia. Even though I had been presenting as male outside of school, I never really encountered any hostility with my gender presentation. However, I knew the sort of people who were at my school. I had been bullied before and I knew that nothing would change and it probably would only get worse for a while. Aside from being unaware about anything trans (or LGBTQ) related, as most teenagers are if they haven't come across the subject in real life, my bullies would have yet *another* reason to torment me. They would think that their comments of 'man' and 'beast' were justified: here I was, a manbeast or some other kind of weird intersex being that they had always thought I was. A lesbian, a male impersonator, a drag king. It was all the same to them. Many of them didn't even know I was transgender. When they saw me in my male uniform in January, they thought whatever they wanted to about me.

What my teachers didn't realise is that when you are harassed or bullied by people you've never seen, don't know or spoken to, you can't get their names. You can't ask for them, and you can't ask their friends. When I went back to school as Jon in my male uniform, the most trouble I got was from the immature students in the younger years, as most people in my year had some idea already due to the fact that I had started to come out to a few people. They were mostly OK with it, apart from a few. The comment that hurt me the most was from a boy in the same year as me, who happened to be a friend's friend. The comment went something along the lines of: 'Don't touch me you tranny, you all have AIDS.' It must seem so tame compared to death threats and other verbally violent abuse many trans people face on a regular basis, but from someone who I thought was generally all right, who knew my own friends, that was a blow. And the viciousness of the comment stood out amidst the sea of 'tranny' and 'man' and 'dyke'. This was wilful hate. I reported the incident and never spoke to him again. I was asked inappropriate questions too, about surgery. I wasn't even on hormones at that point, and had barely cut my hair! But I took this in my stride. When asked by one boy, who I had received a fair deal of harassment from, when I was going to get anything done I replied, 'I can legally have surgery when I am eighteen in the UK, and I will probably start testosterone then too.' He stood there and openly laughed at me in the corridor, in front of everyone. His words didn't hurt me, what was hurtful was his assumption that I wouldn't do it.

This harassment gave me even more resolve to progress with my transition in spite of all of the negative and vicious comments. I came back from my first day at school as Jon and made a video diary about it for the documentary. I haven't watched it in a while, but I remember being resolved and determined to muddle along through the negativity. I don't think I realised at that point that people like to recycle their insults; every day, every time they see you, they need to reiterate the same tired insults, 'tranny' or 'dyke'. These comments, however ignorant or immature, would grind away, anger me, hurt and frustrate me. The majority weren't as vicious as the 'AIDS' comment, nor were they particularly witty, they just happened *a lot*. I don't think I was prepared for my self-esteem and stamina to be eroded in such a way. I guess I had expected that if there was going to be any hate, it would be quite a hoo-hah and a big thing and, as such, not difficult to report to the teachers, who would deal with it well, and I would find it easy to get it over and done with.

There were funny moments though. I was coming out of school one afternoon when some boy decided to shout that I was a 'chick with a dick'. *That* was brilliant, and it's a good example of how kids like to spew insults without truly knowing what they are saying. I guessed that one of their friends must have pointed me out in the courtyard or around the school one time and said to him 'It's a tranny', and I must have passed as male so brilliantly, that he thought I was a pre-transition trans woman!

As with the bullying I had suffered before, I kept many of these incidents to myself, or played them down. I thought I could deal with them by myself, which I could. Through my affiliation with QYN I knew how to deal with transphobia at school and who to speak to, and not to be afraid of reporting incidents and seeing them through. I was confident talking to teachers, staff members and heads of years if I wanted to report an incident, and I kept an incident log, which I gave to them at the end of each week. I tried to log down names for this purpose, as well as date, time and place. I knew that if I wanted to be taken seriously then I had to make sure people knew it was a big deal if they abused me. They had to know I wasn't a pushover, and they had to know that I was an actual person and not some novelty freak they could feel free to target. I tried my hardest to make sure they were dealt with appropriately, whether that was exclusion or detention or whatever. I felt it was important for them to know there were consequences to every abusive comment they made.

Actual questions about my transition were few and far between but it was clear who was curious and didn't know quite how to phrase things properly. I couldn't put it out there to everyone that if they had

questions just to ask me respectfully. I had no plat-
form; I couldn't just announce in the middle of lunch
that I was happy to answer anyone's queries about
what I was going through.

I just dealt with things as I had always done: alone,
albeit with a little more faith in myself, and I didn't
resort to any self-harm or self-deprecation. I had
stopped harming myself when I came out of hospital.
I had trans friends who were going through the same
stuff, and some were having a worse time than me,
which actually made me feel a little better about my
situation. I knew who I was and I didn't beat myself up
too much about it; I was starting to become proud of
my identity, despite other students telling me I was
wrong or unnatural or a freak. I was part of a vibrant
and close-knit community. I wanted to emulate those
who I saw speaking out against transphobia and who
weren't afraid to stand up for the person they were. I
had also come a long way since my first rumblings of
gender discontent – all that now seemed like a long
time ago. I had transitioned this far, and I couldn't
stop or go back now. I had already made the first huge
steps into feeling more comfortable within myself,
and the world had to feel comfortable with me too.
And if they didn't, they could keep quiet about it. I
wasn't going to be a doormat. I wasn't going to live
like that; I wasn't going to allow it.

I would swear back at the harassers when I could, although I tried not to. One time I got into a fight with someone, for which I received a week's internal exclusion. The fight, if you can call it that, didn't go in my favour at all, and I was promptly put in an embarrassing headlock for the entire corridor to see. The boy had said to me that 'sex and gender are the same thing', and he wouldn't take no for an answer. If I was having that same conversation with him now, I would have tried to explain that of course it isn't, everyone knows that, and when he didn't get it, roll my eyes and leave it there. I don't know why I decided to run after him and jump on him. Maybe I'd just had a long day. Maybe it was the straw that broke the camel's back. Whatever the reason for my anger that time, it was out of character, and I've never got into a physical fight since. I am not a physically aggressive person and the reason I behaved like I did was because of the overwhelming frustration I felt. I still have problems with confrontations and anger, even now, although I'm really not much of a fighter: I'm five foot four and skinny, so it doesn't stand me in good stead for anything physical.

Writing was a great help to me, as it always has been, and was now my preference to taking out anger on myself. Apart from venting about my day on blogs, I wrote down terrible things about the people tormenting me – death-threats, the horrific things I wanted to do to people who made my life hell – things I didn't believe in doing for real, but getting rid of my aggression on the page felt good. It was a release.

I didn't tell Mum just how bad things really were; I think at the time I didn't realise how bad things had become, I just told myself that it wasn't *that* bad. I guess that I didn't want her to think it was the wrong idea for me to transition at school. I didn't want her to think that I regretted it, that I couldn't deal with it. I wanted her to think that I was prepared for all this, even though I wasn't. But it *was* bad. It shouldn't have happened to me; it shouldn't happen to anyone. Only now do I realise that the verbal abuse I received wasn't just 'playground banter', it was much more serious than that. The remarks that made me break down in tears, the relentless grinding denial of who I was, the rude questions, the ever-present snide comments, all these things were bullying and I just thought it was *normal*. It was *normal* for me, a freak, to receive abuse and harassment from the other students. I suppose I felt that I had to accept this for the change I had made. And maybe I also believed that the abuse was really my fault for transitioning at a place where I knew there were going to be a lot of people shouting at me and whispering behind my back. That's the dark side, the other side of my feelings about coming

I looked as though I had swallowed a watermelon.

Big eyes and squishy hands at five months old.

Mum and me (the bald one) in Peru.

Three generations - grandma, mum and I.

I remember the feel of tucking my trousers into my Welly boots, all 'toastie' in the snow.

My first day at play school, I felt very small.

In my favourite summer dress. I felt pretty and loved my pink jelly shoes.

My badge was for helping younger pupils to read; I've always had a love of reading and writing and these became a coping mechanism in my teens.

Mum took me on a surprise trip to Disneyland, Paris.

Up north in my comfy jogging bottoms.

I tried my hardest to be *normal* in my 00s clothes!

As Willy Wonka for World Book Day in primary school!

Me pre-transition in my mid-teens ice skating in London.

Wearing a hairy hat, forked beard and my *Korpiklaani* – epic Finnish humppa metal band.

I love my son now as I loved my child then, and that is unconditionally.

out at school. On the one hand a fierce pride and defiance and wanting to hold your head up high. On the other, the niggling and almost ever-present thought that maybe it's all your fault anyway, that this is what you deserve and you should just sit down and shut up.

The school had an obligation to deal with any bullying that went on and my case was no exception. As I've already mentioned, I would report the occurrences of bullying to the relevant staff members and they would do what they could. I would feel hesitant about persisting in finding out what action had been taken, even though I longed to know what my harassers had got in punishment. Usually, I didn't find out at all and I just hoped that they had been given detention. When I couldn't find out names of harassers and so couldn't report them I just hoped that they would abuse me again but in a place where I could easily access a member of staff. In the end I relied on the CCTV cameras to capture any faces – I'm not sure if they were ever used, though. The act of reporting the instances of verbal abuse became as monotonous as the abuse itself, but I knew I had to keep at it. I couldn't let it go. I was still sceptical about how the school dealt with bullying in general; I knew that bullying and bad behaviour was a persistent problem, and nothing had ever really changed since I'd started school in Year 7. If anything, the kids were getting ruder every year. There was little sense of control, even though the staff 'did their best'. However, I felt put out and dejected after I saw that the 'best' I was going to get was a try. Not the crackdown on bullying I'd hoped for.

Although I was disappointed, I should really be grateful. I have heard horror stories from other schools where the headteacher openly blames the transgender student for somehow inciting the hatred towards them, and refuses to deal with any abuse, verbal or physical. I could have been refused any form of protection; I could have been refused the right to transition to male in school full stop. However, I thought that since they were going this far in allowing me to be visible as a trans person, and that they wanted to deal with the abuse I was getting, they should as well try and go the full way and start discussing LGBTQ issues with the students and educating them on the issues. This, in my opinion, would have been a far, far better way of dealing with the abuse that I was getting, rather than dealing with it by only tackling each incident as it happened. I longed to speak to people, to educate them about my gender dysphoria. If I could organise an assembly or a classroom visit from a support group, if my fellow students could have some small awareness of me and who I was, and be presented the facts of gender dysphoria, maybe the hurtful ridiculous comments would stop? It seemed worth a try. At the very least it would open a few minds and allow a forum for students who had genuine questions, but were too unsure to ask them or didn't know me well enough. It would halt the endless surgery-based misconceptions (and they would soon find out that 'chick with a dick' is not the best insult to use for a trans man).

Was I allowed to do this? Fat chance. My mum and I had given the school information on support groups and organisations that will go into schools to work with students and talk about diversity issues. But I was attending a school with a Christian ethos. I was told that parents could complain; what would the governors say; was it really necessary for the students to have this sort of education? For crying out loud, I *never* had any useful sex education at that school. I don't think anyone did, apart from watching videos of nude human beings in science, and seeing a penis getting erect. I learnt everything I knew about sex and sexuality from the Internet, or porn. I would see in the PSHE (Personal, Social and Health Education) textbooks pages about sex, maybe even catch a paragraph about being gay. No chance of us discussing those issues in class – we had tedious lessons about healthy eating, banking and the government. I remember that one time we did cover the various types of sexually transmitted diseases. We had to research them and present them to the class. But I can't remember a teacher telling us how to *prevent* the STIs. I know that in RE there was a page in a textbook about homosexuality and Christianity (Lisa and I used to love this page as it had a picture of a rather attractive priest on it). We never discussed that page in class, and we only covered that topic in A Level RE, which I took. It was an unfathomable impossibility that now they would suddenly start talking about LGBTQ issues. Trans issues were definitely not on the school agenda.

It was immensely disheartening, but I at least thought things would get better in the sixth form, that maybe people would be more LGBTQ aware, that perhaps if the school wouldn't, then *I* could do things. I took inspiration from other schools' sixth forms and colleges, which had anti-homophobia posters and celebrated LGBTQ History Month, and from the Gay Straight Alliances in the USA – perhaps we could have one here.

I started back at the sixth form, already a few months on testosterone by that point. For a week during the summer holiday leading up to our start back, the prospective sixth formers were invited to the school to take some tester lessons and experience life there, as we were to be the school's first sixth-form students. In the summer, around a month before I actually started back in September, I was still at an awkward in-between stage in early hormonal transition, where you don't pass quite so well, but are still read 98 per cent of the time as male. I had longish hair and a very androgynous face. I also had no suit to wear, or even my own tie, which set me painfully apart from the other boys who had had suits, ties and shoes from formal occasions since they were young. There were new students, too, people who didn't know me. I prayed that I wouldn't be outed, but I knew that it was likely that I would be. People were still not used to my new identity, and although the people attending the sixth form day were in my year and generally smarter than the rest of the school, there was the possibility that one of them would say something they shouldn't. And it would be no end of awkward: I looked and sounded much younger compared to all of the other boys, who had had testosterone coursing through them for years whereas I had only been rubbing a packet of gel on my skin every night since April. I had become shy around boys; now that I was passing as one most of the time I felt that I had to be like them – being shy was for girls and I didn't want be a shy guy. I would be presenting myself as a doormat once again if any of the new students wanted to have a go at me. I wanted to have the chance to be, as naff as it now sounds in my head, 'one of the lads'.

Before starting hormones I had 'butched up' in and out of my male school uniform in order to compensate for the lack of physical masculinity and passing ability I had. I thought I had to drop all my effeminate gestures and traits if I wanted to be taken seriously as a guy. If I cared so much about being a 'true man', I had to act like one at least. Many trans men camp up the manliness, and many trans women act more feminine than perhaps they feel in order to be taken seriously. This is of course not necessary; one shouldn't have to act like a stereotypical man or woman in order to be seen as one. Cis gender people don't do it so why should trans people? Those who knew me then and know me now may find it hard to imagine that I ever even attempted to 'act butch', but I did. It wasn't really me but I was so scared about not being taken seriously as a man, that I tried to fit in as best I could at the time.

In a lesson one day I spoke briefly to another guy and I could hear my own voice taking on a completely different tone from how I normally spoke. I had purposefully made it deeper, spiked with a bit more attitude, but quite 'matey' at the same time. I quickly realised that I probably sounded stupid, like a female in a pantomime who was playing the part of Peter Pan and who was trying her best to put on a boy's voice. My voice was squeaking and breaking around that time, so I didn't know what was going to come out of my mouth anyway, a butched-up voice or something else.

No questions were asked of me from the new students and I don't think they knew I was transgender, or a girl, before. Well, no one ever mentioned it to my face anyway. I tried to assert myself in those mock lessons as much as I could, often using my knowledge in a few subjects to gain some approval and projecting the image of a nerdy guy. If I couldn't be a stereotypical manly guy – I soon gave that up; it really wasn't me and I felt more relaxed as a nerd – I felt comfortable in knowing that I was being read as male. However, there was always this fear in my head that at any point it would all end and I would be outed as an impostor.

One time I was nearly outed by a friend. She and I were going to class with a new guy we had just met. I can't remember what we were talking about, but I'm not sure if it had anything to do with gender. Everything was fine, then, from out of nowhere, came her joking comment that I used to be a girl. The new guy was confused and he didn't really know what to say. I just kept quiet. I couldn't believe my friends would treat this information as a joke, and that I could be outed to anybody. I was silently angry but I didn't tell her that I resented her saying that – I let it go. However, nothing of that nature ever happened again.

When I joined the sixth form in September I knew

that I was going to be out to the majority of the people I went to school with because of the Channel 4 documentary about me. I didn't mind this, but I knew that people had to respect that while I might be different from the other boys in the sixth form, I wasn't less of a person. Seeing the physical changes hormones had given me, I felt comfortable in knowing that no one would think of me as a girl anyway. I looked radically different, facial hair had started to grow, and I had an even deeper voice than in the summer. If anybody maliciously called me a girl, it would backfire as I would be read as male by every student in the school, old and new.

I went back into the sixth form as Jon and looking completely like Jon, but being out in the public eye as transgender. The reaction I got from the students when I started in September 2009 was overwhelmingly positive. I owe this to the fact that I made (if I say so myself) a good documentary! No one seemed to have anything bad to say about it or me. I didn't get any comments, apart from good ones, which made a change. No doubt students new to the sixth form knew who I was, as I got congratulated and people talked to me about it, but no one treated me any differently from any of the other guys or used my female name or a female pronoun to describe me.

Now that I had asserted myself as a male, I could be

true to who I was and not put on any masks or voices to make myself appear more masculine. I would be an out and proud, quite effeminate, pansexual man. If anyone wanted to attack me, they would harass me because I was openly not straight, not that I was transgender. I could deal with the homophobia as it meant my gender was accepted.

There was one thing that disappointed me though. The person who had been my worst abuser, and was also overtly racist and homophobic, was allowed to join the sixth form. That completely threw me, as I thought I would never have to see him again as he wouldn't be coming back to the school. I knew that other pupils were as shocked as I was. It wasn't just me, there were other victims he had bullied who were also now in the sixth form, and victims he continued to bully in the lower school. I felt deeply uncomfortable, but I never broached the subject with any of the staff as, despite knowing of his behaviour, none of them seemed to make an effort to control him. I, however, was determined not to be a victim any more. I was now well into the beginning of medical transition, and I was accepted by the sixth form. My documentary had been positive and successful, and I was happy with myself. I was no longer the shy tranny who still looked like a girl. In my new suit and tie and meticulously styled hair, I thought I looked handsome. If he wanted to remain being the person that he was, then so be it.

I remember a time in the sixth form when we were allowed out of school for lunch. I was waiting at the bus stop to go down to McDonald's and this particular boy was there with a boy he had befriended from the new sixth-form intake. He decided he would be clever and witty and call me 'Natasha'. Of course, I had no reply for his stupidity any more; I gave him a withering stare and told him that, for the last time, my name had been legally changed and if he so wished he could see a deed poll. Legally I wasn't that person any more. I knew he would never understand though, so I just plugged my headphones back in and went back to waiting for the bus.

So my transition in the sixth form was never an issue, and it was never really talked about. I was always Jon and read as male, and even read as male by those who had refused to see me as anything but female at first. As my physical appearance changed more and more, people started becoming more accustomed to the transition. Did they take me more seriously now that I was going through some sort of medical process? I think so. I think that if I had remained pre-T (pre-testosterone), then I would just look like a girl wearing a man's suit – to many people it would look like I was pretending to be a man. It feels like medical transition with hormones or surgery is seen as the only way to transition; the only way to have a valid identity. I hate the term 'sex change' as it's been used in every sensationalised media I can think of and gives the impression that sex reassignment surgery is a quick fix. These days it is often substituted for the term 'gender realignment'.

I do think my transition in school would have been received very differently had I not done the documentary: I had no opportunity to speak to people about being transgender otherwise and I think my transition would have been more confusing to more people. I am lucky for the opportunity and experience I had; I at least had a chance to explain to people about me, about Jon. Many trans people have to explain themselves over laughs and jeers, or hastily and vaguely before possibly being insulted. In my case, people watching the documentary about me were sitting down in their own front rooms, listening to my story in comfort, and with me a comfortable and safe distance away from them. It gave them a chance to think about what they had seen. It must have made some sort of a difference, because in the sixth form I didn't have to go through the shame that I had experienced in Year 11.

I left the sixth form in 2010 before I completed my first year. The reasons were unrelated to gender; I never saw myself staying on, and even though I did well I felt the need for a change. I wanted to carry on with my volunteering, I wanted time to help other people and to think about the direction in which my life was going, and I felt that school was stifling me. I started volunteering at PACE when I dropped out, and helped to plan the youth group activities and write the newsletter, giving me far more work-based experience which I believed to be more useful than qualifications at that point. Although things had been relatively smooth in my transition at sixth form, I did feel disillusioned regarding LGBTQ awareness. I was upset when the school powers that be said it was too risky to let Years 7 to 11 acknowledge Worlds AIDS Day, as some of the more conservative parents would not feel it was appropriate. To not talk about LGBTQ people is one thing, but to veto mention of AIDS because of its association with gay sex is another. I managed to get a few posters up though, and made sure they were placed well in the view of students so I did my part. I don't know if they have changed their view since. For the improved education of their students, I hope they have.

Luisa: My coming out

During those first few weeks after he came out to me I didn't tell anyone about Nat being Jon. I needed time and I just focused on our initial steps towards getting him support and referrals. I was in a suspended place. I was going through the motions of a daily routine: wake up, have a wash, get dressed, go to work, work, train home, stop off for food shopping, get home, change into house clothes and so on. I felt like a sleepwalker, I was awake but part of me had shut down. It was probably a good thing at the time, it was a way of coping and dealing with the situation without going into an emotional overdrive. I kept life as simple as I could; my focus was my child's well-being. We kept as normal a routine as possible, Jon continued going to school as Natasha and getting through the school day. Some days were better than others. The most important thing was that he knew that at home he was loved and accepted. I held on to this, hoping that this would get him through to the next stage of his transition. It did.

As the mother of a transgender person I had my own coming out to do. Writing this makes me realise that I had no idea what Jon was going through at that time and I never will. I know it must have been a tremendous relief for him to tell me about his 'secret', but how many other emotions and feelings must he have gone through too? The hardest thing is that I will never know what it is to be fifteen and go through what he went through – I can never share that with him. As much as I was there for him, there were places I could not reach and be a part of. It is hard for a mother not to be able to take away the pain their child feels. As a parent you want to make it all better, for the pain to go away and for everything to be all right. It is hard realising that you cannot do that because some of that pain they have to bear on their own. All you can do is love them through that pain.

Work

My first coming out was at work. I told my boss and line manager. I felt this had to be my first step because there would be days that I wasn't myself and if this impacted on my work they needed to know why. If I needed to take time off for appointments with Jon, I wanted that to be in place too.

I spoke to my line manager first, who has always been very supportive. Another colleague was in the room at the time. Both people I consider more than work colleagues, they are friends. Their initial reaction was of disbelief, not disbelief that what I was telling them wasn't true, but disbelief that I was having to deal with this kind of situation. I explained what I had done so far in terms of arranging treatment and how I was doing emotionally. They were both caring; it was a relief to tell someone in the outside world about what was happening in ours, and to experience a positive reaction. I then told my boss, who was also very understanding. Explaining my situation was not as overwhelming as thinking about telling it, and it felt good to take part of that weight off my shoulders. I left work that day feeling a tremendous sense of relief. I knew that there were still many coming outs to go through but this was a good start. Yes, it was a big thing for others to take on board but take it on board they could. It was not about understanding gender dysphoria, it was about accepting it. I still had a lot to learn in order to come to an understanding of it, but it is separate to your acceptance of a situation. The most important part of coming out is that people accept that it is the truth.

My brother

I had not seen my brother for some years, not since the death of our mother. We had both held her in intensive care as she was dying, having made the painful and difficult decision to switch off her life support machine. She died at one minute to midnight; it was her birthday. Our filial relationship has never been the same since then; we grew apart, with anger and hurt on both sides. We talk on the phone but there is much that is left unsaid. He is my brother and I love him and I hope that one day we will be able to bridge the distance between us.

It was around a month before I could tell my brother about Nat. He listened; I could hear the deep concern and disbelief – 'Surely this can't be happening?' – in his voice. He was very caring, he has a good heart. He has always asked about his nephew's wellbeing every time we speak on the phone and speaks to Jon on the phone too. He wrote Jon a very loving letter once I told him and has always kept in contact. I have sent him photos of Jon but he has not met him yet. I hope that this will happen soon.

Jon's father

I feel disappointment, anger and a deep sadness that it is the way it is now. We have our opportunities in this life and we can choose to miss them. Jon's father I feel made that choice.

To me his father's great loss is my great gain. To deny your child is to deny part of your existence. I will say no more on this as it is too painful.

A family up north

I am thankful for the continued contact of my ex-husband's family. I told Jon's auntie about him being transgender and she and I both felt it best for her to tell Jon's grandmother in person. It was going to be difficult for his grandmother; she has always wanted a granddaughter and deeply loved Natasha. She is a woman in her eighties and has gone through hardships in her life. Diversity and change is a difficult thing for her to accept, as her life has been limited to her own community and I understand that. I can understand that for her generation, our world is one that they are uncomfortable with and at times scared of. There were tears, shock and incomprehension, which were only to be expected. Yet her continued love for her grandchild is a mark of my respect for her. She could not watch the documentary and has never been able to bring herself to. When we first spoke about Jon she was honest and said that it would take her time to think of her granddaughter as 'he', so for the time being she would write to her and talk about her as her 'grandbairn'. It would take her time.

She now writes Jon on his birthday cards and when we have spoken on the phone she has referred to her 'grandbairn' as Jon. She has shown that, regardless of our social and cultural backgrounds and upbringing, we can all make the changes and choices that we know are right in life, as different and as difficult as these may be. She has not met Jon yet, I don't know if she will, but she has the time and choice for that. What is important is that she still loves her grandchild.

Jon's auntie has been only what I can describe as a tremendous person. She accepted that Nat would become Jon. Although initially she was shocked, and it was difficult for her to understand gender dysphoria, her first response on me telling her the news was one of support for us both.

Jon's family up north have shown us that even when life is difficult to understand, what is essential is the capacity to continue caring. They have my on-going respect for doing that, and it means a lot to the both of us.

My Spanish familia

I seemed to do a lot of coming out all at the same time. Once you start it sometimes feels right and the best way forward to continue. It is also a great personal relief and helps you to move on. You think, well, that is one step out of the way, now on to the next. It does empower you and you learn who is there for you and who is definitely not. The Spanish side of my family was next. Although I am bilingual, explaining about transgender in another language was going to present its problems (it's difficult enough explaining in plain English!). I am good at colloquial Spanish but the more technical words were going to be difficult. I called my cousin Azu, she is a teacher and a linguist and has a good knowledge of English. She is also one of my favourite cousins. She was fab and took it really well. I did my TexMex (Spanish with a smattering of English words for the bits I found difficult to explain linguistically). How the gods smile down on one sometimes – who knows the reason but their timing is crucial! That conversation was such a time. Azu said that she would tell the family face to face, and a large family of aunties, uncles, cousins and second cousins it is. One of my other cousins, Susana, is a journalist and while I was explaining to Azu that my daughter was transgender, she was writing an article on gender dysphoria and had just interviewed a local transgender support group (unbelievable that there is a transgender support group in a northern Spanish city that is conservative and focused on the café society lifestyle! You could not make that up if you tried). I sent them Jon's new passport photo, which was taken to get him his new passport acknowledging his male gender. I received emails and phone calls from my aunties telling me he looked handsome and that they were there for us if we needed help and support. Jon and I were so comforted by this, it was an amazing positive step forward for us both.

It had been three years since we were last in northern Spain to visit our *familia*. I felt it was now time to go again. Jon wanted to; he wanted to meet the family as Jon for the first time. As I was now in a relationship I wanted to take my partner Russ to meet them. It had been ten years since my divorce and this was my first serious and meaningful relationship. Russ and I met through friends. After years of feeling lonely I met a man who cared for me through my good and bad times, who valued the meaning of companionship, who gave me his love. I talked to Jon about our trip. Would he feel more comfortable just the two of us going over and then at a later date I would go over with Russ? Or did he want all of us to go over together? He felt it was best (and I agreed) that we should all make that first trip over together. He would not feel as if he was the centre of attention as much if Russ was also there. I agreed that it would take some of the emotional burden off him. So we made plans. The *familia* were really looking forward to meeting Jon and Russ, and we all had a fantastic time. We felt that this first trip back would be best kept short – it was going to be intense for all – so we only went over for four days. The family welcomed Jon as though he had been Jon to them all his life. A beloved uncle of mine who is a diehard traditionalist shook Jon's hand when he first met him, and then gave him a warm tight bear hug as though he had known this nephew all of his life. They all said that my child had such courage, that they respected his decision and that there was such a marked change in the person they met. No longer a shy, awkward, uncomfortable girl but a young person brimming with confidence and warmth. I had been anxious and nervous for Jon. When I told him how I felt he had reassured me he said that he was looking forward to it and that I should not worry. I am so proud of this son I have. Russ was his usual larger-than-life self, and was the charming and warm, loving person that he is. He has always given my son support and help when he has needed it and has always been there for him. In Spain he was mindful of Jon and his well-being, he was mindful of me and towards the end of the stay, as I was getting emotional and tired, he was there supporting me. For this, and for so much more, I love him.

Maybe the acceptance of Jon in Spain was because the family had not seen Natasha for such a long time. So the next time they saw her she was Jon, a very different person, and because of that it was like meeting someone for the first time without the difficulties of seeing him transition. By the time Jon went to Spain he was well into his physical transition and looked so very different to the young girl that they remembered. I think this made it much easier for them; they welcomed him as a young man.

The absence had been a positive thing and it felt like a new beginning for us all.

Friends

You learn who your true friends are in times of need. I have two good friends, Carina and Julia, who have given me their support, time and care. We met each other through our children going to the same primary school, and started casually talking while waiting at the school gates for our children to come out. Our friendship developed slowly, their children coming over, Jon going to theirs. They fully accept that my son is transgender and respect him for the person that he is and respect me.

Others who I felt were friends fell by the wayside, unable – or unwilling – to cope with someone else's problems in their lives. You get frustrated waiting for the phone to ring, hoping that they will be at the other end to support you. Just a little of their time to ask how everything is going. When they don't, you feel angry because you always have to be the one to contact them, and you feel guilty that you are taking up their time and being overdemanding in wanting their support. These emotions go round in circles. Eventually you learn that if the phone does not ring it means that they do not want to commit their time and, frustrated as you are, maybe you need to realise that it's time to let go of that friendship. It does leave you feeling desolate, isolated and let down when people you felt close to suddenly stop calling and eventually disappear from your life. You feel like shouting at the world because they are not listening.

What is important are your true friends and their true friendship. Even though I do not see these friends as often as I'd like to, I know that they are still there for me. Even if I called in the early hours of the morning in a time of need, they would do their utmost to help me, as I would do the same for them. Time does not change that with friendship.

Six
Gender and Everyday Life

Jon: Then and now

Many people think that 'gender' and 'sex' are the same thing; that they can be used interchangeably. I've had many a heated debate with people who vehemently claim that this is true: they think they are different words for the same thing and that your body and biological 'gender' is who you are, and sets you up for life. But there *is* a difference and one that society overlooks time and time again, causing no end of confusion to trans people. I still have my share of frustration when I am asked for my 'sex' on forms, even though my sex is now male.

The difference is simple: 'sex' is your biological make-up (your genitals, what the doctors assigned you at birth – male, female or otherwise), 'gender' is what's between your ears (what you perceive and feel yourself to be). There are many theories on how a person's gender is formed, by nature, nurture or a combination of both, or a reaction to society or absorbing what people tell you you are. However, many people experience a strong misalignment between their sex and what they believe themselves to be mentally. This incongruence between your body and your gender perception is called gender dysphoria, and it's what most trans people usually have to some degree; the feeling that your body and mind don't match up.

The problem with wider society viewing 'sex' and 'gender' as interchangeable was, and is, a problem for me pre- and post-T. Pre-T – or pre-testosterone – I usually didn't know what to put on forms that asked for my 'sex'. I didn't want to put female, but I felt like I was lying if I put 'male'. According to my legal documents, my sex wasn't male yet and I certainly didn't look it, even if I had acquired a little 'M' on my passport (I got this after a few months on T); you can get your passport and other documents changed at any point in your transition as long as you have a note from a medical professional. I, like many trans people, didn't know if I was breaking some law if I put down my preferred gender when they asked for sex. I knew they were different, but when they put down a category for 'sex', did they actually mean *gender* too? And if they are using sex and gender interchangeably, then could I safely put 'male'? I was confused, but I just put male on everything I could, smiling with relief when I was asked instead to put 'gender'; at least I knew I was doing something right if I put male there. I never got pulled up about it, but the few times I've been in sexual health clinics I have stalled over what to label my 'sex' as. I remember one time I went in for a check-up and my referral sheet asked for sex, and I was stumped. *I have a vagina – should I put female, just so the nurse or doctor doesn't get a shock? And what if they send me to a male nurse if I choose to put male, thinking I have typical cis male genitalia?* Being unashamed in testing different organisation's inclusivity about trans people whenever I can, I asked the receptionist what I should put down. He looked confused at first, but I explained to him that I had been born female and consequently didn't have the male genitalia. He said it would be fine for me to put male down on the form, as the nurses aren't geared towards one gender or the other. That was after only a few months on T, but even now, over three years on, it still happens. I still feel awkward because of the fact that my body is anatomically different from that of other men.

I do feel that this should be irrelevant: who is

anyone to tell me I have a 'male' or 'female' body and at what stage does, in my case, a female body become male? Is it a male body when I think of myself as male, is it male when I look male and have body hair, is it male when I get a mastectomy or a phalloplasty? Am I never going to be male? I have heard some people say that no matter what I do to my body I am 'never going to be a true man'. Whenever I hear this I think that if someone passed me in the street or served me in a shop they wouldn't think to question what was below my belt. It seems that when some people find out that I have differently formed genitals from what they expect, they deliberately seek to alienate me by saying things of this nature. If I hadn't disclosed my trans status to them, they would never have known anyway, and would have continued to treat me as male.

I don't like it how something as fickle as mere biology defines who we are. Something that is irrelevant to who we identify as: our personality, our soul and our mind. All of these combine to create something that far surpasses our physical make-up. I think it's unfair that a person who identifies as male but doesn't fit in with the ideals of society then has to change their own perceptions on the diversity that is life. There is a wide biological variety in cis men: fat, thin, large chests, skinny chests, small penises, large penises. Why shouldn't the bodies of trans men simply be another part of this variation too?

To feel like your body is the wrong sex, that everyone sees you completely differently to how you see yourself, is an alien feeling. If we all just took time to place ourselves in the shoes of a transgender or gender-variant person, then I think more people would begin to understand. An exercise commonly used in equality and diversity training is this: if you woke up in the body of the opposite sex, how would you feel? Some common things that come up are feelings that something isn't right, that other people don't see you for who you believe yourself to be, disgust for your body and how it insults your mind, anger – burning yet blameless – for being assigned male or female, frustration at society and the world for being binary centric and boxed in a black hole. When you wash yourself you take care to not look at those secondary sex characteristics which 'give away' your biological identity that you try so desperately hard to hide and make false but they are so irrevocably there that you have to make conscious decisions not to even touch or to look or to think about them. You quickly learn to disassociate yourself from your body and live only through binding or tucking, or clothes and make-up.

So you put on those gendered clothes and go out

into the street and sometimes, or a lot of the time, get 'sir'-ed or 'miss'-ed in conflict to how you identify. And it feels like all your hard work is for nothing. You fail to 'pass' as your gender; you fail society's test.

It's agonising. Agonising the first time, agonising the second, and it is still as painful when it happens the hundredth time. It wouldn't feel *right*, or *natural*, if you woke up in the body of the opposite sex, because your mind would still be your true gender and that wouldn't change no matter what clothes you dressed your body in.

That's how it felt for me, before transition. It felt awkward and wrong stepping out every day into a society that refused to acknowledge or mistook my gender presentation. The dissonance between my body and mind, my soul and what people perceived me as was painful. It felt like I had to be the best actor in the world to pull the wool over people's eyes, and make them believe that I was truly male. An actor and not simply a human being who was just dressing up in clothes to fit their gender. I used to overcompensate quite a lot and I ended up, as many trans guys do, looking like a butch lesbian. I wore cut-off shorts, cut my hair stereotypically short and wore striped polo shirts and Vans. More often than not, people in the street or who I met didn't comment (I guess because I looked like just another butch lesbian?) but I didn't take their silences as positive and I didn't want to talk in public for fear my female voice would give me away. I was paranoid that people were looking at me, that the word 'dyke' would be whispered behind hands and that I would be laughed at, singled out, humiliated. I wouldn't be able to say anything back in my defence, because who was I kidding? I looked nothing like a boy! And lurking at the back of both my and Mum's minds was that ever-present and serious threat: would I get beaten up?

Mum had heard the horror stories, as had I, about trans people (usually trans women) being the victims of hate crime, sexual abuse and vicious hate-fuelled murder. A few incidents happened in the UK, but the majority of them were in Mexico and the USA. She'd heard from another parent who had a transgender son that he had been beaten up at a New Year's party for being trans. She was right to be concerned, however, I never did fear much for my own safety. Maybe I was too young and naive to take my personal safety seriously. I never thought it would happen to me, as I had run into many dodgy people on late-night buses and trains back from London and I was always quick to avoid a confrontation with someone stronger than me (i.e., everyone). I've always thought I really should have been beaten up by now. The amount of bad situations I've been in – young, underage and extremely intoxicated, wandering around some place near but not-quite-so-near my house – is considerable. The times I've stumbled around Soho, Charing Cross or Camden blind drunk are embarrassingly frequent. More so in my adolescence than now; I was rather a wild child around the age of sixteen – I had just discovered drinking, and went out on the gay scene to clubs in Soho where I could get in with my friends. But I have never been in a physical altercation because of someones transphobia or homophobia.

I don't like the word 'passing'. It always feels wrong to use when a person is trying to be perceived as the gender that they feel they are, as if they are deceiving people in some way. To 'pass' in a cis-normative society is to blend in like them, to tick all the boxes of stereotypical gender presentation and be quiet about your trans status; making the body that you are hiding away conform to the expectations of everyone else. To 'pass' is a wonderful feeling. Finally, after so much trying, you are read correctly! But for me, looking back to pre-T, it was a grim satisfaction – you've passed a test, a test set by a cis-normative society to grade you on how 'normal' you look. And it's on your shoulders to do all the work. Once again, you are expected to be the great trans 'actor'. It's up to you to make sure people perceive you correctly and not the other person's fault if they do not. I now prefer the word 'perception'; it takes the blame for 'not passing' away from oneself and relies on how others see you and refer to you (albeit, not always in the correct way).

Nowadays, I just blend in. I am taken as a (usually straight) young man. The beard helps with the credibility. In everyday situations, I'm not read as trans, even in trans spaces. I'm not read as trans in the respect that I 'pass' as a cis person very well. People will comment that they 'would never have guessed'. I find that to be an awkward compliment and I'm never really sure how to respond. I usually end up saying, 'Yes, I know.' When I do reveal my trans status, it's because I feel it's necessary or because I want to. The privilege I have now, being three years post the start of T, is that I am 100 per cent read as male, unlike pre-T where the majority of trans guys are perceived as ambiguously gendered. I am not outed by other people and I don't have the more noticeable awkwardness of being 'obviously trans' or 'obviously androgynous'. If I'm not out and talking about it people just don't know. I am proud of my identity as a trans person and I want it recognised, but I am not going to announce it to everyone I meet in every situation! If the conversation turns, as it sometimes does, to transgender people, I feel the need to out myself then just to make sure the other person or persons know that any comments they make will be directly affecting me. Usually, when

I out myself in this way, people are respectful, if a little shocked. Sometimes people ask questions, but I have realised not as much and not as abruptly as pre-T. Again, it's credibility. There is no doubt that I am male – I appear completely and utterly male to them. Pre-T, I felt like I was treated as a sideshow when I outed myself, that I 'wasn't a real trans person' and therefore people thought they had a right to ask extremely personal questions. Although I do answer people's questions about my gender identity if they ask politely or aren't invasive, and I enjoy talking about it, I won't randomly out myself as sometimes it can make me feel uncomfortable, depending on the person who asks me. Most people have found out about my transition through getting to know me. Some people who knew me before, through and post transition still haven't talked to me about it, even though on social networking sites, I am quite open and vocal about my trans status. Perhaps they find it awkward or rude to ask, or perhaps they just accept it? I think people who I talk to online find out by absorbing and making sense of everything I post up about my gender and my transition, and just muddle through as they get to know me. I don't usually come out to people as trans who have already got to know me relatively well, or who have met me a few times and I hadn't mentioned it to them soon after we first met. I think I would find it awkward, especially if I don't know if they have already found out somehow, through social networking or the documentary. Similarly to coming out as gay, coming out as trans can change another person's perception of you. I haven't had anyone think less of me when I came out as trans to them, but there is always a possibility of that happening. You just don't know.

The thing with coming out to 'everyday people' or being generally noticed as being trans, is that you always need to be ready to explain yourself. You may not know everything about being transgender, and you may not be fully read up on trans issues, transition and medical procedures, especially if you are only just starting to figure out your own gender and do not know your own path. Being a walking gender encyclopaedia can be tedious, especially if you want to be stealth, or if you feel you're passing well one day. A simple, 'So, not to be rude but what are you?' can haunt you for days afterwards and can shatter your self-esteem. This is because trans people are still seen as an oddity in some people's eyes and some people ask personal questions that no 'normal' person would get asked. Also, due to the sexualised nature of how trans people are portrayed, 90 per cent of the questions a trans person will be asked will be about their genitals. These questions usually revolve around if they have them or not, or what they have and if they've changed them. The surprising thing is that some people who you barely know, or may have only met for the first time, feel that they can ask you about this as if it's an acceptable topic of conversation! Many people assume there is only 'the op'; a magical operation, just one, that defines what that person now is, and one that is always to do with the genitalia. Some people believe that a trans person is not their identified gender 'until they've had the op'. Many trans people who 'pass 100 per cent' (like myself) haven't had any ops and unless they specifically come out, no one would be any the wiser. Trans people are relegated to their bodies: a mix of nips and tucks, hormonal changes and 'mutilated' body parts. To many people, and in the media, we are solely transgender beings, our being trans is everything and all encompassing, we have no lives outside of ops and transphobia and as such are weird people who don't work, eat, watch television or do normal everyday things. Sometimes I feel that people have forgotten that I can actually be something else. And sometimes even I forget I can be something other than a living embodiment of transition and gender angst. It's a huge part of my life, but I also like to read, surf the Internet, and stay up late eating pizza and YouTubing. I'm not just a weird transgender body; I have a mind as well.

I think that nobody has the 'right' to question trans

people on their bodies without their permission. People can question but whether or not you'll get an answer is another thing. Some people may just be curious, but it's easy to just use some human decency. If you really want to know something, think about *why* you want to know. Is it really necessary to ask that person specifically, or can your inquisitiveness be abated by Google and without hurting feelings?

Many, if not all, pre-transition trans people have to deal with this fascination towards them no matter the situation. We are walking curiosities, free to be asked 'what's in our pants'. It feels like, to society, we are only 'successful' in our transition; only true human beings, who deserve respect, once we look like a normal part of society – when the trans man has a beard and a deep voice, and the trans woman is feminine and beautiful.

Sex and sexuality is another thing I get commonly asked about, as if gender identity and sexuality are linked. The most common thing people assume is that I, as a trans man, am a 'closeted lesbian'. Gender identity is how you perceive your gender: if someone feels like they are male, irrespective of their genitalia or what society forces them to be, and they only like women they are straight. They are a straight man, not a lesbian. Sexuality is who you are attracted to, and has nothing to do with if you are transgender or not. Some transgender people are gay, some are straight, some bisexual, some pansexual, some asexual. I think the confusion stems from the fact that people still have a hard time viewing trans people as anything other than their previously assigned gender, that they're still a woman or a man, *underneath it all*. I am not a 'woman underneath it all'. Underneath my clothes is a body, underneath that there's a mind, and all of it is male. None of it is anything close to 'lesbian' – although I dabbled when I was younger I couldn't be one now if I tried. My sexual identity has matured and I identify as pansexual now, so even if I identified as female I wouldn't be a lesbian. Another misconception is that all trans people, once transitioned, have to like the opposite sex: all trans men have to be attracted to women, and trans women vice versa. Interestingly, I know more queer trans people than I know solely straight trans people (so much so, that it's a novelty and a shock when I meet a completely straight trans person; trans man especially)!

My liking for men can sometimes come as a blow for those who say I'm a closeted lesbian, and people who adhere to this belief don't get how I can be a mostly gay man and transgender. Do they think that other gay men find my body repulsive and weird? No doubt there are some gay men who might find my body repulsive but those are the sort of men I would not want to be with. All of the men I have slept with have respected me as a male person, even with my different genitalia. I am strong enough to demand respect in the bedroom, and if I know a person is going to be uncomfortable or not understanding about that then I won't take things further with them. What I am comfortable doing in the bedroom changes from person to person. Before T and social transition, I was more sexually adventurous. In my 'wild child' stage of drinking and socialising I could genderbend more and it was easier to sleep with queer women and queer men. (Trickery? I don't think anyone cared.) Now, after T, my genitals look extremely different (I remember my first serious long-term sexual partner didn't know how much the clitoris – my penis – changes on testosterone and got quite a surprise the first time) and so I can't really have one-night stands on a whim. Many trans people who haven't had any surgeries often need to out themselves if they want to have sex with a person who expects a different, more conforming, set of genitalia. In these situations, it's best to prepare for the worst. Most times it's unavoidable, yet necessary, and can be disheartening; another reminder why you just can't be a 'normal' person who can enjoy nice things. Since T, the only people I've had sex with have been partners who've been trans themselves and so have understood and accepted my body.

The level of body comfort in sex varies from trans person to person; I personally don't like vaginal penetrative sex, but some trans men do. I don't mind not having a penis equivalent to a cis guy's; other trans men get very dysphoric about that.

Some people view trans people as sexual deviants, who transition purely for fetishist reasons, or to get into specific people's pants. This comes back around to linking trans people with sex: it feels like everything trans is related to sex and we can't have 'normal' sex lives. I'm not comfortable in divulging the finer details of my sex life here – but I will say that it's satisfying, and I do have it. I use the parts I have, some people may use toys or additions, but that doesn't make trans people different from anyone else who has sex. Many people use strap-ons or other enhancers, regardless of gender identity.

Many trans people, at the start of their transition, need to face the dilemma of how to react to 'not passing' in public, especially when you are misgendered. If someone misgenders you do you correct them, do you let it go with awkwardness and shame or do you just accept it? It's a tough choice, and people may deal with it differently or differently on different days. It's good to have friends who stick up for you if misgendering happens in public. At the beginning of my transition, this was a huge confidence boost. I remember there was always a feeling amongst my trans friendship circle that if someone got your pronoun wrong, in and out of the group, there would be a conscious effort to correct this. This happened on multiple occasions. I was on a bus back from a protest and one guy just didn't seem to get that I was trans, like many people he perceived me as a very butch lesbian. There was a quiet reinforcement of my pronouns in every sentence by my friend ('Yes, *he* is coming with us afterwards', etc.) and I felt good that even though my friend was a cis guy, he respected my identity enough to consciously correct other people.

I often felt I should be able to correct all sorts of people myself, as a matter of securing my own pride – often a simple 'I'm a guy', usually worked and I don't think anyone ever denied my identity to my face. I passed reasonably well in LGBTQ space, and no one seemed to question my gender if they had just met me in a youth or social queer setting. Maybe this was because everyone I knew was exposed to trans men, and knew that if he was short and dykey, he was probably trans and to use male pronouns. I also remember tearfully correcting a policeman on a train (tearful because I had PMS and was frustrated, not because of the misgendering), and also shakily affirming my gender when I was stopped at a men's fitting room.

Changing rooms. Now, apart from toilets, these are the gendered spaces that really got to me when I was first starting to transition. I was once asked if I was a guy or a girl, despite the men's item of clothing I was holding. (Seriously, I just need a space to put on these jeans without the policing!) It was the only time I got stopped when going to use the men's changing rooms – but I was allowed in after I said, 'I'm a guy', to the shop assistant. I knew my rights anyway: I was all ready to quote the Equality Act and that I was not allowed to be discriminated against as this counted as 'providing a service', but I didn't need to. It can be a disheartening experience, especially if it's a first time buying men's clothing. A few months ago – I'm not sure whether this is a remnant from my past – I found myself asking for the directions for the men's changing rooms in a shop. Not the changing rooms, but the *men's* changing rooms, as if I was afraid that they were going to suddenly look past the beard and deep voice and direct me to the women's changing rooms instead. I suppose, due to my internal sense of dissonance from cis men and my general history, that I will always be trying to affirm my male gender in one way or another. Pre-T, the level of how comfortable I was in affirming my gender or correcting people usually relied on the amount of alcohol in my system. In the middle of a night out I was much more likely to swagger into the men's toilets than I was when shopping during the day.

Other times when I was out and uncomfortable using the men's toilets, there would be encouragement from my support group friends and 'toilet buddies', who are friends who go into the toilet of your preferred gender with you so you do not have to face the peeing, and sometimes hostile, Joe Public alone. I know from my experience as a toilet buddy for other people that telling them to walk quickly and confidently into the toilet and to stare right back at anyone who looks in their general direction can sort out any unwelcome curiosity in the men's.

If there's one thing that can be uncomfortable and upsetting, it is the fear of being confronted in the toilet. This fear can range from the sense of paranoia, internal shame and wrongness to a fear of having to speak, to show yourself up. Gay bar toilets, especially, can be a nightmare for the young trans guy who often gets mistaken for a lesbian. I've had friends forcibly barred from using the men's toilets in gay bars, friends who have been harassed by drunken strangers and followed into the toilets while the toilet attendant did nothing. I myself have been questioned in a gay club by the toilet attendant, however, it was after I finished peeing so all was good. I ended up explaining to him (for quite some time, according to my drinking buddy)

174

that I was trans and a guy, although he said he was sad because I should stay a girl. I was drunk and so gave him my number. After a few sleazy texts later on that night, I never spoke to him or saw him again. I'm thankful that this is all the toilet-related drama I've had to deal with pre-T. I don't often go gay clubbing, for the good reason that I find it shallow at the best of times, and at the worst of times racist, sizeist, sexist and transphobic. Gay clubbing was me at sixteen, nowadays my big night out is a meal at Nando's.

I was in drag for London Pride two years ago (drag, as in bright red lipstick, stuffed bra, high-heeled thigh-high boots and a bondage dress and leggings, complete with beard and eye shadow). Ever the gender benders, me and one of my friends (also in drag) decided to touch up our make-up in the men's toilets at Victoria Station before we got on the tube to Baker Street. Feeling giddy, we both went in and proceeded to do our make-up. The stares were brilliant. Especially from a cleaner, who just stood there in shock for the duration of our make-up session, clutching his mop. I heard a guy chuckle, catching sight of the cleaner's wide eyes, and he said, 'Well, what can you do?'

Even though being seen as male 99.9 per cent of the time is pleasing for me, it's good to switch things up on an occasion like Pride. Besides, make-up and thigh-high boots are brilliant, whatever gender you identify as. I was ecstatic on the march, I got so much attention and even got invited to a VIP club night. My advice if you have low self-esteem is to dress up in drag. You feel fabulous. The only thing I'm worried about now is that I've set the bar so high for me looking and feeling great in drag that I won't be able to match it.

After Pride I used the men's toilets when some friends and I went to Hyde Park for a chill out. I went in, confident that I really wasn't going to get anything more than a couple of weird looks for my now smudged make-up and bra (I had removed the high-heeled boots), and because I had a beard I thought no one could really say anything. I was wrong! I was accosted by a man, who insisted that I was in the wrong toilets. I said that I was a man. I thought that would do, after all I have a deep voice, so surely he couldn't possibly . . . No wait, according to him I was still in the wrong toilets. I sighed. I was then dating a pre-T trans guy, who was behind me, so I had to get this man out as quickly as possible. I looked my accuser straight in the eye, raised my chin, pointed at my face and said, quite specifically and flatly, 'Mate, *I have a beard.*' He looked at me, apologised, and left. Although, perhaps that was because some park policemen were standing behind me in the queue. Other than that occasion, I have not gone out in drag with a beard (something I must rectify, it really is as brilliant as I claim it is) and so have not had these extraordinary experiences with the general public.

'Tranny bladder' is the term used jokingly to describe the syndrome of being able to hold in pee for long amounts of time, due to an aversion to using public toilets. (Although the word 'tranny' should never be used to refer to a group of trans people, *even* if you have trans friends who say it is OK for you to refer to them as that, you should never think that all trans people are OK with that word; it's still used as a slur, and can be hurtful.) I don't have an STP device (stand-to-pee device), so in men's toilets I always need to use the stalls. This is fine, if say you are in a train station or shopping centre where there are quite a few stalls to choose from, but not so good if you are in McDonald's and there is only one stall. I was waiting for what seemed forever the other day for the stall to become available, getting extremely odd looks from the people peeing then leaving (What?! Maybe I needed to do a number two!).

I prefer using accessible toilets even now. They are gender free and you have much more room; I used them almost exclusively in early transition, when I could. However, I always felt guilty using the accessible toilets, I always imagined coming out of an accessible toilet and having someone in a wheelchair glaring at me as I sheepishly walked out. One time I was at the theatre and I was waiting for the accessible toilet to be made available – my friend had gone in before me – while two women stood waiting in line behind me. After a while they asked me why I was waiting for this toilet when the men's was freely available a few metres away. Of course, I had no logical answer – I had no visible need to use this toilet, and obviously I had passed to them. (I didn't ask them why *they* needed to use the accessible toilet, seeing as they appeared as able-bodied as me, but I am not one to make assumptions.) I sheepishly turned around, acted in surprise, as though I had just realised there were male toilets there, and went in. I was post-T then, but still, being directed to use a certain toilet brought back some nasty memories.

I know that trans people don't have to justify toilet preferences to anyone, but it feels like you always need to have some sort of excuse at the ready, to justify your appearance or why you are in a certain toilet. The justifications can vary from hormonal imbalances, to growth problems and late puberty, to genital piercings and disability – anything but mentioning that you are trans.

Concerts were an interesting time for me, and one situation where I didn't mind a bit genderbending. Pre-T, I nearly used to always present as female when

I went to concerts. One of the reasons for this was because it would be a social situation where I would be in close contact, and speaking, to other people who may not be exposed to queer and trans stuff, and so would be much more likely to misgender me when they heard me speak and talk about how hot all the men were. I'm a metalhead, and even though most people are fine with LGBTQ stuff I wouldn't chance being out as trans pre-T at a Dimmu Borgir or Slayer gig. As stereotyped as it seems, I find being 'out' as a metalhead pretty hard, as it tends to be a 'macho' and quite heterosexist environment. However, there is an interesting story of me pulling a bisexual guy at a Slayer gig in 2009 after I told him I was male. It was a bizarre experience, one of luck more than judgement, I think. I was in a queue and he was drunk. (On second thoughts, that may have had something to do with it, but we did hook up sober, too.) After joking around with him, he asked if I was single, and I said that I was male and that I was underage (it was two weeks until my sixteenth birthday). He apologised for hitting on me under the age of sixteen, but also said that he didn't mind that I had said I was male. A little while later I met up with him for drinks in Camden, and he's always referred to me as male. But even since that experience, I continue to complain about there not being enough openly queer people on the metal scene. I did present as male at some gigs though, especially when I revealed my name. (When asked for it at gigs, I often stumbled and said 'Jon', even though I knew I probably didn't pass.) Surprisingly, open transphobia has never been a problem for me at a gig. I've had some funny looks in my time, but I have never been confronted about my gender. I remember one time when I did say my name was Jon and got a slightly terrified look from a drunk guy at a death metal concert. Another time, I outed myself as transgender in the queue (when one queues for eleven hours you get to know people and talk with them a lot), and got nothing but support and understanding. I would first introduce myself as 'Jay' and then as 'Jon', preferring to test the waters with the neutral name Jay. I needn't have worried, though, they asked me why the hell I hadn't introduced myself as Jon in the first place, and did not find me weird and abnormal as I thought they would. I have also been proved wrong when addressing the problems of misgendering for a friend of mine at another gig I went to. I was tipsy, and so felt I could deal with it, and told the person who had been 'she'-ing my FtM (female to male) friend, that he was really a 'he', and if he was OK with using male pronouns. He said that of course it would be fine, and used male pronouns from thereon after. No talk of trans issues, just acceptance. I still find myself surprised when everyday cis gender people are so tolerant after hearing all the horror stories of people dismissing other's gender on a daily basis. When you find someone who just accepts, it's refreshing.

I also presented as female at most of the gigs for the female privilege that is being a groupie. I still miss that dearly, being the fanboy that I am. I doubt many of the sexy, long-haired men would want a short, scruffy eighteen-year-old English queen warming their tour bus beds! (One can dream!)

However, pre-T, I used to doll up for gigs like there was no tomorrow, in hope to impress some gorgeous rock musician and that he would fall hopelessly in love with me (and to outdo all the other girls! Rawr, claws out!). I would go all out, and stuff my bra and wear low-cut tops and short skirts with big boots, looking fierce and alluring at the same time. I went to a concert in Germany with my mother (this was after I had come out to her, but I was presenting as female for it). By some unspoken understanding, when we introduced ourselves to the band, she referred to me as her daughter and as Natasha. I didn't mind at all – I was surprised she'd got it spot on! I milked my femaleness for all it was worth – hugs, coy questions and even presents (I mentioned it was my sixteenth birthday and after the gig my mum came back from the pub laden with free signed merchandise for me). I could never do that now unless they were gay or very drunk. Now, I'm perceived as an extremely gay guy, which gets me no presents from any band! Oh well, some things you need to give up. Looking back on it, was I inadvertently promoting sexism when I used my sexuality to my advantage? I didn't think so: as a woman I had enjoyed flaunting my figure. It made me confident – I was confident at that gig, far more confident than at any gigs where I'd try to present as male pre-T, and as a consequence appeared shy and awkward. Sexism is a touchy issue, but I believe everyone should enjoy using their sexuality however they please, as long as it doesn't hurt anybody. It may have got me the wrong sort of attention at that concert, but hell I *enjoyed* the attention. I enjoyed this act of positive discrimination. It got me things. Invitations to bars, drinks . . . and if I wasn't interested in a guy, I felt I was strong and feisty enough to fob him off. Would I use my sexuality to get me things again? Sure, why not? It's something I feel I can take ownership of, trans-bodied or not. I think sexuality in general, and using it, is something that is seen today as very taboo, especially for women. Why should it be? Nowadays, it is seen as 'dirty' and not something that can be wholly positive.

People have asked me about my views on sexism, and if men and women are treated differently in society and my experiences of that. Of course sexism exists, you don't need to have experienced a social transition from one gender to another to realise that. Previously, as I have said, I could use my 'femaleness' to get me things, from dodging train fares to getting good customer service from men and things done quicker. This is still sexism – women being treated differently just because they are women – but certainly when I was presenting as female I sure as hell didn't mind it! Beauty, also, has a part to play in this. I never did consider myself attractive as a woman, despite what others may have said, so I didn't really have much experience in getting things done for me by men. Other friends of mine, stereotypically attractive friends, have. That's just the way society works. But I was able to get away with being coy and pretending not to understand as much, so that I could sometimes use this to my advantage. If I was out and about, I could play the damsel in distress, and act shy and sweet (such as a woman is supposed to, ugh). Unfortunately society still sees men to be intrinsically assertive and more sure of themselves. That old fallacy of men not asking for directions or help is partly true: as a man in society, you don't want to seem weak. That is a terrifying burden that is placed upon men, and one that I certainly felt in transition. I felt that more was expected of me because I was now a man. I couldn't be the coy woman who could ask for help and receive it when needed, no one was there to help a man. I suppose in that respect I feel pressured, and somewhat of a failure. I did feel as though I needed to live up to typical manly expectations; I needed to put up shelves and have an excellent sense of direction and I needed to learn how to drive – all of which I cannot do. As a woman, I felt I never needed to do any of that, I didn't feel that anything was expected of me. I guess this was because I was a teen and as women get older there are as many pressures for them as well, such as their appearance and the notion of having it all – being a wife, mother, career woman and domestic goddess! That's still a display of sexism by society and society's views on a woman's place, but I *enjoyed* not having a burden. I should have been more concerned about it, I suppose, and I do now consider myself a feminist and a campaigner for gender equality. But in my adolescence, playing the damsel in distress, amid all the tribulations I was going through with depression and hospital, was a relief.

As I previously mentioned, I never thought I was a good-looking woman. On the contrary I usually thought I was ugly. So I never really had that to flaunt, or would hear men make comments about my looks. When it did happen, instead of feeling disgusted, I felt flattered. It was a rarity that someone found me attractive, what with my curly, untamed hair and all.

In that respect I have never experienced looks-based sexist remarks. I have never been called a 'bird' or a 'fittie'. I think the extent of my female experiences has been the expectation that I couldn't look after myself as much, and that it was more valid for me to ask for help as I was a woman. However, as a man my looks are noticed. I consider myself a relatively attractive man now, and have been noticed and eyed up by a few women on the street (as well as by men). Again, I feel flattered. I suppose I'm still not used to it. As a man, I cannot use my looks to get me things the way a woman potentially could. In my experience men are more likely to do things for women they find attractive, more so than women doing things for men they find attractive. As someone who likes attention, and affirmation that I am good-looking (perhaps still a fear that I don't quite 'pass', that somehow if women don't find me attractive they can somehow sense my trans history), this is bad for me. Deep down I just want people to be nice to me.

Society also has another card to play when creating barriers for me: I am not a 'typical' man. There are many flaws that society sees with how I present and how I think as a male-identified person. Apparently, once you've started testosterone your map-reading skills are meant to get better. I've heard (I have no idea if this is true) that there have been reports of trans men becoming more spatially aware and, rather amusingly, better at parking than when they were not on T. However, I think my sense of direction has got worse. I always get lost, am always clumsy and not good at maths. Being an atypical man, especially a trans man, does attract sexism and hassle as well. Gay men and effeminate men and men who cannot do 'manly' things are *still* seen as less than men because of their feminine qualities. Gay men are portrayed as men who wear women's clothes and who only associate with women, and who talk about clothes and shoes. They are still men, but less than men (as it seems that liking 'women's things' makes you weak and inferior); a different gender altogether. And as a trans man, that does lower your credibility. If you're 'such a man' then why are you gay or effeminate (linked in many people's minds as the same thing)? Many people think I am camp because it's 'funny'; I find this insulting. I still find I have to reiterate the point to people: there are many types of men, and there are many types of trans men – *and we're still all men*. Some men are camp, some trans men are camp. Some men are butch, some trans men are butch. We're all men, some just happen to be 'trans'.

I am sometimes perceived as gay, sometimes from my mannerisms or how I talk about certain topics, and I have had homophobic remarks made about me, but none when I was presenting as ambiguous pre-T. I don't mind these remarks; I'm out and proud, and enjoy presenting as flamboyant and camp and wearing nice clothes. It's just the man I am, and it doesn't make me any less or any more of one. I think that my mum is now more worried that I'll get beaten up for being perceived as gay rather than because people know I'm trans. But again I haven't been beaten up so far, even though I've been in some tense situations. She hasn't questioned me about my sexuality or got confused, as far as I know, about my gender identity and my sexuality. When I was presenting as an ambiguous butch female I wouldn't get active abuse; a man wouldn't go out of his way to start on me because I was masculine, or threatening their masculinity by identifying as one of them. Now, men (and it's always men, the only ones who I've received any sort of homophobia from) think I'm an easy target because I am a feminine man; a disgrace. God knows what they'd think if they knew I was trans as well! I usually get hassle when I've been out wearing make-up (usually not a lot, just a bit of eyeliner, which isn't that abnormal nowadays). Anyway, the few incidents where I've got abuse haven't put me off: I think looking fabulous is more important than shying away. I've overcome transphobia in school, and I can come out as a mostly gay and flamboyant man in society and deal with any remarks I get. I'm not hiding who I am any more, whether that be my gender or sexual expression. I also think it's important for trans people not to feel they have to conform to gender stereotypes in order to be taken seriously: the more trans men who aren't afraid to show that they are feminine, the more gender, and trans identities in particular, can be explored as part of a spectrum and not outside the binary one that is so predominant in our society today.

Homophobia can occur within the 'trans community'. I haven't personally experienced any hassle from within my community because of my presentation or sexuality. I have a number of trans male friends who are not straight, but there does seem to be a need, perhaps from cis-normative society's pressure on us to constantly 'man up' and prove ourselves, to talk about women, to be the macho straight man. I know some people who've experienced homophobia from within. I think this is bred out of fear – the fear of difference, when you are already so very different yourself, the fear of people showing the community up for anything other than 'masculine'.

I still feel uncomfortable with 'male interactions' in society. I don't know if cis gender men feel this way, but there is a level of awkwardness and underlying coldness in male social interactions that I don't feel with women. On the whole, I feel safer socialising with women, but I do enjoy conversations with men. As I got older and started to become interested in more typically feminine things, I felt awkward talking about these things – clothes, men or make-up – with other guys. It simply wasn't done, and as a man in a conversation with another man you both have a burden to have a good, manly conversation. I never think I live up to other guys' expectations; I am, and always will be, slightly socially awkward. I think it's the forced chumminess and the onus on everyone to keep the conversation to a level where everyone is comfortable. I know that I like feminine things, that I am expressive and have a varied range of interests, and that I'm slightly shy and geeky, but if I am having a conversation with another man I usually feel I can't be my true self. I need to be assertive and sure, and make jokes that people will actually understand. I need to work at a conversation. I've always found conversations with women to be easier on me – I don't have to try as hard. I find that as a man, there's some inexplicable pressure to always be in some sort of competition with another man, to be better or cleverer or more interesting. I find this difficult as I don't want to be predatory, and I don't want to censor what I talk about. For me, there is also the fact that I am gay, and inevitably, or in my experience, there is always some mention of women *somewhere* in the conversation. There is usually a mention about a girlfriend or something. If I am having a conversation with someone and I want to say, 'Ohh yes, my partner has such and such, he thinks blah,' I can't. Especially if the other person is a man. There's still a stigma surrounding it: you cannot tell if a person, especially a man, is going to judge you for mentioning a same-sex partner. I mentioned the other day to a group of people that I volunteered for a 'gay organisation'; the mood in the predominantly male space shifted, I felt awkward, and somehow I could see that I was viewed from then on as 'other' than a man. I went on a hairdressing course a while back and mentioned that my interest had been piqued by cutting an ex-boyfriend's hair and the mood stayed the same, with light conversation being made. There was curiosity, but absolutely no hostility. I guess society generally expects men to be more homophobic, and more transphobic, than women. I don't know if this is true, but I have experienced a different atmosphere surrounding sexuality with both genders.

To my mind, friendliness comes more naturally to women; with men it feels forced. I detest being called 'mate', I simply hate it. Especially from men who I don't know. It is usually when they want some-thing and I, being ever socially awkward, don't like giving people things in public. I think, when the term 'mate' is used towards you, there is the assumption that you are a 'mate' kind of guy – a manly type of guy, an average Joe, a bloke, a geezer. And thus you have to act accordingly, and be 'matey' back, again a burden of expectation. As I'm not a 'matey' person at all, I always feel as though I am acting when I am in an interaction with another man. It feels forced, it feels weird. Maybe this makes me less of a man. I don't know. I just know that I tend to find it easier talking to women or more sensitive men. Maybe this is my past coyness and yearning to be the damsel in distress showing through. Maybe I'm just an awkward guy.

It's odd coming from a place where you don't fit in outwardly, to a place where you still don't fit in. Transition, and even social transition, can make a person feel better about their gender, and in turn, it can make them more confident. People have noticed a definite change in me, that I am more likely to speak in public, whereas before I would be shy and uncomfortable for the majority of the time. However, I don't think I've become more confident in myself. Being 100 per cent socially male now, I feel I should be outgoing, confident, and open to speaking and giving opinions. Inside, I'm still an outsider in many ways and I still don't feel comfortable. I think many men, cis men even, also feel this way but I haven't had a deep conversation about feelings with a cis guy (stereotypical,

I know). I think I'd like to, I think it would be good for men to talk to each other more – it would abate the feelings of inadequacy and 'what a real man should do'. Men could stop trying to hide so-called 'unmanly' aspects about themselves. Just my two cents, as a socially awkward trans guy.

Luisa: Folding boxers and sitting on trains

As Jon started his testosterone treatment in 2009, the physical changes he was undergoing slowly became apparent. He started losing the soft round-ness to his face, his bone structure became more defined and his Adam's apple became visible. Facial hair! I remember the excitement in Jon as he came rushing downstairs to show me those first few hairs on his chin. I too was excited for him but it was also a reminder that at some stage I would no longer see my daughter's face in his. His female body was now being pushed to do what it always should have done – go through a male puberty.

Jon's voice broke and deepened. The first time I realised how profound a change this would be was when I called him at home and was taken aback to hear a male-sounding voice on the other end. I knew it was going to happen at some stage but it was still so unexpected. There had been a couple of months of his voice ranging from a deeper tone to the uncomfortable squeaks of a pubescent boy. It was slowly changing then all of a sudden it had happened. For a moment I felt unguarded but at the same time also a sense of intense relief that his testosterone treatment was working.

There was so much unexplored territory that I had to journey through. Sometimes I could just stride ahead, dealing with all the changes I encountered. Other times I felt lost and very alone in a bewilderingly unfamiliar landscape, feeling as though all the progress I had made, mentally and emotionally, was fragile. It would feel like I had gone round in a circle and was back at the beginning. Even now, three years on, I still have fragile moments. Transition means going through changes, being in one space then another, mentally, physically and emotionally.

As difficult as it may be to understand, my coping mechanism was – and still is – to keep it simple. This is the journey I am on now, and it is as it is, as simple as that. I cannot change that I am in this space, what I can change is how I deal with it. I cannot make a situation go away because it is not on my agenda or outside of my comfort zone. What I can do is not dissect feelings, fears, thoughts and what ifs. Down that road lies a mashing-up of my brain cells and I don't need that to accept what is happening now.

Keeping it simple works for me. I can assure you that at times simplicity is the most difficult thing to hold on to, but it is what has been the most positive way for me through difficult times. Simple tells me that my child is going through profound changes. I too will go through profound changes. I cannot alter that. Change is not easy; what is easy, regardless of all my feelings, fears and anxieties, is the one simple truth that is eternal for me, and which is above all others: I love my child and this love holds no conditions.

I would sit on the train to work cautiously studying the faces of young men around me. It was important for me to compare Jon's changing face with their masculinity. I wanted him to be able to sit opposite someone on a train and for them not to question his gender, that they would look over at him and just think 'young lad'. It is amazing how preconceived ideas of masculinity and femininity are challenged once you start looking closely at strangers' faces. I observed young lads with soft feminine features, women with big hands, others with hairy arms, some with large feet. Men who looked androgynous, women with heavyset facial features, girls who could be pretty boys. Short men, men with small hands, women with defined jaws. Men with little facial hair, women with thick eyebrows, tall slight men. What struck me was the gender fluidity in so many faces and bodies. This certainly helped to ease my anxiety that Jon would not 'pass' in this everyday world. That people would look at him and guess that he had been born in a female body. Thankfully, though, Jon did pass in this external world of stereotypical gender recognition; he was a slight and good-looking young lad.

Another worry, and a continuing one, is his personal safety. That on a night out with friends he might get beaten up by other men when he went to the 'gents', or by women. All parents worry about the safety of their children; mine is compounded by my child being transgender. I worried and then worried some more, fearful for his safety, anxiously awaiting a text from him on his nights out telling me where he was or that he was on his way back home. If I did not hear from him I would imagine the worst, a call from Accident and Emergency, a police officer knocking at the front door with 'I have some bad news for you.' Feelings of sick dread waiting up for his return were made harder waiting alone as a single parent.

Hanging out the washing I would catch myself thinking 'I am hanging out boys' clothes to dry' – a simple statement but a complex thought. I remember the strangeness of folding boxer shorts. Only strange because it was so far removed from what I had known and done before, I was used to hanging out knickers.

The first time I bought Jon a pair of boxer shorts I took a pair of his knickers with me! I had no clue as to sizing. Odd to be standing in a shop with his knickers against a pair of boxers so I could find the right size. For his first birthday since beginning his transition I bought him some clothes. When I went shopping I automatically went straight to the girls' section. There was so much unlearning and relearning to do. I realised that from now on I would be shopping for Jon in the boys' section; it was a strange feeling, yet somehow important too. I asked the shop assistant to pass me down a shirt that was hanging right up at the top. I remember having a compulsion to tell him that today, right now, was the very first time I was buying a man's shirt for my son, and to explain that this was because he was transgender. I did not act on that compulsion, there are moments when we do share with strangers but this was not one of them. I suppose what was essential at that important moment was that I was proud of my son and I wanted to share that pride and to voice that I also felt pride in myself; this was a big step for me.

With the emergence of Jon's physical masculinity

came all kinds of changes. The bathroom window-sill now had shaving gel, men's razors and aftershave on it. It felt very odd seeing these. Odd because it had always been us two girls with our girly things scattered around, so to now come across these male objects seemed very out of place. I had been divorced for seven years and hadn't had a relationship in that time, therefore, there had been no male presence visible. There is now.

I have a son.

Seven

The Boy Who Was Born a Girl

Jon: Show the truth

Starting out on the shaky legs of transition, not many sixteen-year-olds would feel comfortable being filmed by a media company for a documentary. Not many would have the opportunity – what are the chances of it happening on the cusp of the beginning of the rest of your life? An ideal moment: a film crew there to capture the pivotal moments of your early transition! But this is what happened to me at the end of 2008, right when I was stepping out for the first time as a trans man.

I hadn't been out very long at all, it wasn't even a year at that point. I had joined a support organisation called Mermaids, which provides family and individual support for young trans kids and teens in the UK. They had given me the opportunity to meet others like me (usually around the same age, some a bit younger) and for my mum to meet parents of other trans kids and to share experiences with them. There were a few of us around the same age in various stages of transition. Some had to go abroad to receive the necessary hormones and to start surgery, as there was no possibility of starting on their transition in the UK. Guidelines for treatment abroad are different to those of the NHS in the UK. In Belgium, Canada, USA and the Netherlands the process of puberty can be suspended before sixteen. The UK is now finally doing drug trials. One of the tremendously positive aspects of Mermaids (and there are many) is that there are carefully organised events that allow families and young trans people to have a safe and supporting environment in which to be themselves. It allows for a space for some of the younger children and those starting out on their journey to be with others who may have journeyed further in their path of transition. Parents can express their difficulties, children and young people can express and be themselves and meet others who can be positive role models for them. Some families find themselves constantly having to explain their child's gender variance to unaccepting primary and secondary schools; some are in a very different position from me who had a relatively understanding secondary school. Some of them have no real support from medical professionals; some are at the beginning of their battles to get help for their children, some are in the middle and some at the end.

Soon after I became involved with Mermaids, a documentary filmmaker named Julia approached the organisation with a view to following a trans child on their journey of transition. Mermaids posted her emails to all its members to see if anyone was interested. I knew the effect that the media could have on trans people and their personal lives. I was aware first hand of families whose personal lives had been cruelly intruded on, reporters camped outside their homes, contact made with people who were willing to sell their stories. I knew when I agreed to start filming that this was something I had to carefully consider.

It was for these very reasons that Mermaids were very wary to take part in any kind of media coverage. They had good reason; this was something not to be taken lightly. As a trans-support organisation dealing with young children, a sensitive and taboo subject, they were approached regularly by media companies with questionable agendas. This rightly made some members unwilling to be involved. Ultimately, it had to be an individual decision. Julia's initial contact message was passed on to all members of Mermaids.

This was Julia's first directing role, and she was interested in making a genuine documentary about the lives of trans children and teenagers starting out in their transition. No one took her up on it, apart from my mum and me.

At first we genuinely thought it would be something quite small. We assumed a few families might take part and our story would be a part of the others. There were a lot of factors, which meant that it might have been better for me to just get on with my transition without a film crew following my every move. We didn't know how big or how successful it was going to be or whether it was going to be shown on national television or not. We didn't know at that time whether it was definitely commissioned. For all we knew it could have been something the bosses were interested in, or they might have felt uneasy about putting it in a good slot. It could be a failure, and expose our lives in a trashy way. With all that in mind, we still chose to contact Julia for a further meeting. I guess Mum and I both had a good feeling about her and her intentions. From the initial email contact she made to Mermaids she seemed genuine enough, and a face-to-face meeting would either put us at our ease or show up some red flags. We weren't going to be forced to sign a contract right away, and we are both strong enough people to turn things down. At that early stage the ball was definitely in our court. We were just curious. However, I think that in the back of our minds we knew that this could be a special opportunity, and something that we would want to see through. Otherwise, we wouldn't have made contact with Julia.

Even at this early stage in my transition, I felt a desire to make a positive change. I may not have been the most learned on trans lore of my friends, so maybe not the best person to speak knowledgeably or lengthily about complex matters of gender identity, but I could empathise and I could talk about my feelings and share my ideas with the camera. I could show others that trans people were normal with normal human feelings, and that being trans shouldn't be seen as freakish, a fetish or a sin. For me, the best possible outcome would be that I could educate people about the transgender experience by just being who I am: normal Jon, who has a story. Thinking big at that early stage was what made me sure that I wanted to at least try and do this, however small a part I might play in this documentary. My mum felt the same. Between us there was the combined thought, *'If not us, then who?'* We couldn't just wait for someone else to do it. If everyone thought like that nothing would ever get done.

Mum and I have always had the same drive and passion, and we knew that we both wanted to do this, in fact, we thought that we should. Looking at everything that could have gone wrong and the months of hard work and exploration that would have been involved, and the possible negative consequences, you could say that we were very foolish to take on such a project, that we should have left it to some older trans person, or at least someone who'd gone through transition a little way. But for everyone involved, and for the people who would eventually watch the documentary, what was important was to follow someone on their first steps; something rare and vulnerable and ultimately important. That would set it apart, that was the integrity of the piece. If done right, then this would be something I would be 100 per cent proud to be a part of.

So in the end, Mum and I decided to do what felt right to us. We arranged a meeting with Julia. We didn't know how events would proceed after that but my mum and I had good feelings about it, even though we knew we had to be cautious. The initial idea that Julia had sent to Mermaids was to hopefully have a few young trans people and their families sharing their stories. As it happens it would not turn out that way.

We met with Julia in 2008, around Christmas time. Mum had met up with her beforehand and she said she came across as really nice. I had been forwarded some emails from her and she seemed warm and friendly.

The first thing I noticed about her was that she was very pretty. You could say I was a bit smitten (not that me finding her attractive had anything to do with wanting to make the documentary!). I remember telling a friend, who also appeared in the documentary later on, how beautiful I found her, and it was an in-joke whenever we filmed together. I pleaded with her not to reveal it! We went for lunch at a café a short walk from our local shopping centre. We must have talked over lunch for a few hours.

I found out that Julia had been inspired to make the documentary after reading an article by a *Guardian* journalist that focused on a parent from Mermaids and their trans child. She was taken with the story and decided to research this topic of trans children and young people. This would be her first time directing, which meant it was challenging territory for her. It was a first for all of us.

Julia said to Mum and me that she had had no prior knowledge of anything to do with trans issues, but that the piece written in the *Guardian* was so moving and inspirational that she had felt compelled to seek out other people's stories. She was doing this for education, like Mum and I were. She was as passionate about getting our stories out there as we were, and wanted to help other young trans people and their families. I knew then that her interest was genuine. I couldn't detect any hidden agenda or hidden motives, she was just a genuinely lovely person, which I had thought would be a rare thing in a media producer making a documentary about gender identity issues. We were on the same page from the outset, with the same ideas about what the project should be. We didn't want this to be tacky. We wanted it to show the truth, and we wanted it to deal with the issues sensitively. Our interests matched perfectly. We discussed confidentiality and what rights we would have: everything would remain strictly confidential and we would have total control of what went into the documentary and what stayed out and how we filmed. Julia assured us that we could pull out at any time during the filming process. But even if I had wanted to pull out halfway through, I don't think I would have. There were certainly times when I felt nervous and apprehensive about filming, but abandoning the project halfway through was never an option for me; it would have just been such a waste of everyone's commitment, time and effort.

This seemed like an ideal situation. We were in total control and we were all in it for the right reasons. Result. All we needed now was the contract!

During that long talk in the café we laughed and

spoke about other things apart from filming. It really was just like meeting one of Mum's friends for a coffee. I left first (I wanted to go and do some shopping), while Mum and Julia stayed and talked. I felt exhilarated about the possible project, buzzing with satisfaction that everything was coming together. I love projects; I think I take on far too many, but I love them. I love working on something, cultivating it, making it my own; especially when it involves putting a part of me into it. I have been involved in a lot of arts projects. I volunteer for Gendered Intelligence, creating art, which speaks about transition and life as young trans people, and also have helped to set up a sexual health clinic for trans people and their partners in Soho. I think that's what I loved about Julia and her initial ideas – this would be about 'me', and another chance for me to express myself to the world. It is important for me to put aspects of myself out there for people to examine and to ask me about. I also knew that my story was in safe hands. I liked her. Mum and I both were left feeling very positive about the possible documentary.

I don't think what we were embarking on really sunk in. There wasn't a moment where I thought, 'Oh shit, I'm going to be in a documentary!' It was never that big a deal. I think the fact that Julia never made it into a big thing was what made it so calm: we were a team, and I think the bond that I developed with her made it 'our little project'. It never felt 'formal' or 'staged', nor was it too intrusive in our lives – having a camera crew in our house gradually became part of our everyday lives for a few months.

In the run up to the start of filming my feelings were of anticipation; I had no idea of what to expect. I knew it would be different from anything I had ever done. Filming would last from late in 2008 until the summer of 2009, when it would be edited ready for a September release date. We still had no real idea what slot we would get on Channel 4, but we all hoped it would be a prime time one so that the message we were wanting to impart through our documentary could be seen by as many people as possible.

The first shots were filmed in my local area shortly after we met Julia. Julia wanted to capture someone on their very first steps of transition and coming out. As I had planned to go back to the sixth form in January 2009 as male she wanted to capture this whole process, from buying the uniform to my first day back. At this point, before leaving school for the Christmas holidays, I had already changed my name at school and got the head of the sixth form to sign my deed poll. The school knew beforehand what was going to take place in terms of my transition at school. At that point, however, they did not know about the documentary. For the meantime, Mum and I decided it would be best to keep it that way. We didn't want the documentary to be compromised in terms of filming, so we would tell the school when it felt right for us to do so.

These initial shots were shown to the C4 bosses. Everything had been set up over the December break, and I remember buying my new uniform in early January. The objective was to film some 'walking shots', and then buy my new uniform, as well as do some filming inside the shopping centre. On my first day of filming it quickly became apparent that I would have to do endless walking shots. I think half of every-thing I filmed was re-takes and shots of me walking down a street. I soon became an expert in walking: it's something that's quite hard to do on cue, to think 'OK, so how do I normally walk?' and not to make it look weird, both in gait and 'neutral' facial expression. I became good at learning to dodge people. When we filmed walking shots we couldn't clear a street like huge-budget film crews could. We had to hope no one would get in the way, but inevitably they did, hence the endless retakes. It was also very embarrassing! To passers-by I was a scruffy boy walking up and down the same street, being watched by a film crew on a grey high street. It must have looked like the most boring film ever produced.

On the first day of filming, one of the first tasks was to film me walking up and down a busy street near the entrance to the school uniform shop where my mum and I were going to buy my uniform. We were to walk past the camera and bus stop and enter neatly into the store. It was a dreary, drizzly, grey day. We also had to be *talking* to each other intently. Not very advanced stuff, but when you're with your mum and doing embarrassing, repetitive activities in front of staring people, it's hard to snap into the mind-set of 'this will be great and necessary'. So, we walked, in the manner in which we were told, trying very hard not to mess anything up. We were miked up, and I asked Julia what she wanted us to talk about. She said that our conversation was not going to be used in the final footage, and that they just needed the shots of us walking, everything would be dubbed over later. So we could talk about anything we wanted to – which for me was as hard as coming up with a neutral facial expression and a normal-looking walk on cue. My mum and me had no idea what we were going to talk about.

'What should we talk about?'

'I don't know, anything.'

'Uh, Nigerian cheese – do they have cheese in Nigeria?'

And so proceeded a whole conversation about how

people made cheese in Nigeria. Having lived for part of her childhood in Nigeria, my mum was surprisingly knowledgeable on the cheese industry in that part of Africa. Of course, this was all on mic and being fed back to the production crew. Nigerian cheese became an ongoing in-joke.

I was relieved when finally we were off the street and into the shop, away for from the strange stares. The shop was a relatively small space, and filming was cramped. I think the shop assistants were con-fused as to why exactly we were filming something as mundane as someone buying his new school uniform. Throughout filming we told people, in the situa-tions where I would interact with them, that we were making a documentary about teenagers growing up and 'coming into manhood'. I guess we didn't tell them that it was a trans documentary for fear that people wouldn't treat me as a normal guy.

After we had finished buying the uniform we filmed inside the shopping centre. None of the shopping centre shots got used though as there were too many people who kept trying to get into shot. This also hap-pened around my local area, a sleepy suburb, with cars slowing down and people stopping to stare. I had to put on my uniform and take a stroll around the block, mimicking the walk to school. For some reason I remember it being very sunny when I filmed these shots, even though I'm sure it couldn't have been any later than January.

In the run up to me going back to school as male I was apprehensive, but I knew I couldn't back out now having come this far in the filming process. Going back to school had been scheduled in, another scene to be shot. We had to edit out all distinguishing features of the school uniform, we got a different tie and I took my blazer off for the walking shots of me going round the block.

My first day back was actually OK. I got some comments, but nothing I hadn't expected. So there was nothing much to report back to the cameras when I came back after my first day, no horror stories, no huge climax. I was given a personal camera, which did get used when things started to take off with harassment and bullying at school – it was a sort of video diary.

The abuse started after about a week back, when the news spread like wildfire and the realisation started to dawn on people: we have a tranny in the school. In those few weeks, following my transition at school, it was useful to sit down in the pink hue (from my pink curtains) of my room and speak to a camera about my day-to-day life with the harassment and quietly affirming my gender. I was still making the documentary even when there was no one there. I found it better, more like me – if I was embarrassed about something sounding stupid, or too simply put, I could go back and change it. The only problem I have with the monologues the crew filmed is that I think I sounded too simplistic. My friends are great thinkers and extremely eloquent speakers; I think I pale significantly in comparison. With my video diaries, I could relate on the emotion of the day as I usually filmed them when I was straight back from school, without changing out of my uniform, the anger or resentment still fresh. In the first month or so, this was most of the filming I did, as well as little shots around the house. Mum was filmed coming out to my aunt, which went very well (I was upstairs at the time, waiting nervously for the outcome). I was also filmed buying binders and looking at prosthetic penises on the Internet. I'd always been able to talk to my mum about sex, and the finer points of being trans. That's always good to have.

Some scenes were staged and some were a natural part of my transition. Some that were staged included me going for a (free!) haircut and shave, which also marked my first shave, and a training session with a man built like the Incredible Hulk. One of the first scenes we wanted to film, and which had to be filmed as part of the start of my transition, was my first appointment at the Tavistock GIC (Gender Identity

Clinic). I think it was probably one of the worst days of filming. I was going to be driven up to the clinic by the crew, from my house on the outskirts of south-east London to Swiss Cottage. Like all NHS appointments it was strictly limited to an hour, and if you miss it or are late for it then you can't get that time back. We got very lost and in the end I was half an hour late and rushed in immediately once I arrived. The session itself could not be filmed, but my reactions to it afterwards were. Julia and the team tried to secure an interview with the head of the GIC, which never materialised. My mum was invited into the session as well, and I sat down with a doctor and had the most vague half hour of my life. We never really stuck to a concrete subject. He asked me what toys I played with when I was growing up (well, stuffed animals, but I also liked dinosaurs and dressing up) and what I expected to get from the Tavistock Clinic ('Hormones, ASAP.' 'All right, well, that won't happen'). It was after the visit that my fears about receiving treatment on the NHS were realised. Even though I had learnt all I could about hormones, time frames, changes and consequences and had gone through counselling, I felt that I was not taken seriously.

I was subdued on the drive home. I knew that it would be mortifying for me to go into the sixth form not having started hormones, or being anywhere near starting hormones. I didn't think I could face the embarrassment and the constant dismissal of my gender because I looked like a girl trying to dress up like a guy. I knew that I had to start taking hormones; I knew this was exactly what I wanted. Like many people who've gone through the NHS I knew what the other option was: the private healthcare route. This seemed to me like 'copping out', rather than soldiering on and getting my treatment on the NHS, but I'd heard so many horror stories of waiting years for treatment and my first session at the clinic hadn't given me much hope. I would have to endure months of 'talking about my childhood', of which, I assumed, mine was extremely atypical to anything a gender doctor would expect from a young trans man. I had not felt any dissonance between my gender role as a young child and my sex, and had not begun to think I might be trans until my mid-teens. I hadn't asserted that I had to wear boys' clothes only or play with one type of toy, and I was afraid that being completely sure of one's gender from a very early age was mandatory to get any treatment.

After some thought and some talking, Mum and I decided we would go to Dr Curtis, a private doctor, and at that time the only private gender doctor in London. One session with him was filmed and he was lovely about it. We also managed to get an interview with him about my treatment. I found him much more clued up and not as 'childhood focused' as the NHS; he seemed more concerned about my feelings, who I was and who I saw myself as, rather than delving into my past to look at the toys I played with.

Within a few months I had started Testogel – testosterone hormones in gel form – which is rubbed into the skin on a large surface area (usually the upper arms). A few months later I was going for my first haircut and shave as Jon. I only had a tiny bit of stubble and I hoped they wouldn't have their suspicions about my delayed puberty and lack of chin hair for a fifteen-year-old boy. It was a swanky place called Pall Mall Barbers off Charing Cross, a far cry from the local unisex hairdressers I usually went to. Having started T, I started to grow my hair out, wanting it long enough to headbang with, so I only wanted a bare trim and a re-shape. It was my first haircut in a barber's which felt like a sort of 'rite of passage', and when it came to the shave after the haircut the hot towel was extremely relaxing, I would recommend it to anyone with the capacity to grow facial hair. The only gripe I had was having to lean forwards into the basin for the hair wash, instead of nicely relaxing back with my head being showered by warm water and getting a scalp massage. The barber explained that this was because women are more likely to wear make-up, and sitting back was so it didn't run. I wore concealer, and I now wear full foundation every day (owing to my bad skin), but I was hardly going to admit that. In fact, the barbers didn't twig that I was trans, and I was happy with my (free!) haircut; I thought I looked a bit like a stylish Wolverine.

After my initial disheartening visit to the Tavistock Clinic, I think my next least favourite moment was filming a personal training session that summer. I'd had no interest at all in personal training, but thought that since it had been booked for me by the film crew, I might as well give it a shot. I am probably one of the most unfit people you could meet: I'm exercise-phobic, I eat junk food more than I probably should, and smoke on occasions. I knew there was going to be trouble when my mum popped her head out of the gym door to look out for the trainer and said immediately, 'I think that's him.' If anyone was built like the proverbial brick shithouse it was this man, his neck was probably as thick as my whole body.

I didn't think, naively, that it would be a proper workout session. I thought that he would take pity on me, seeing my skinny, unhealthy body. No such luck. About half an hour in, after agonising amounts of squats and barbell work and God knows what else, I felt physically sick and exhausted and I left the room close to tears. This was all caught on camera, but if I hadn't left the room you would have seen me impressively throw up on the gym floor. After the workout, the trainer still didn't realise that I was trans, and it was up to me if I wanted to tell him. I was all for the 'dramatic reveal', so I sat him down in front of the cameras, and explained that I was trans – that I was born female. He took it as well as any other person who I'd come out to. He said he had no idea that I was trans, and that he had nothing to say about it; it was what it was, and there were trans members at the gym. He wasn't going to tell me to 'get out'. It was a pleasant experience, and he was genuinely a nice guy. Afterwards, I was offered a present of free training sessions with another trainer up in Camden. I took one then conveniently broke my wrist. I never went back.

Overall there were lots of shots that were cut out. I knew this, but I never realised the extent of the things that wouldn't be shown. In the end the *Big Brother* final trumped our spot, so instead of one hour we were cut down to thirty minutes. There's an extended cut, which features some filming I did at a QYN meet-up in the park. Some filming that my friend and I did was also cut. We were shooting outside a little café in Covent Garden and Julia asked us to talk about the differences in social presentation between men and women. It was a nice bit of people watching, on a sunny day with a cold drink. We were looking at how people presented themselves: the clothes they wore, how they walked, and discussed how we changed or evolved our movements to coincide with this norm.

The only bit with my friend that stayed in the documentary was the talk we had in the park on a bench. It was a grey day, and Julia took us into the park by the back of my house to talk about our school experiences. It was hard for me to get emotional on camera. I nearly did when I divulged the extent of the bullying that had been slowly getting worse. I knew my friend had problems at school too; the school she went to was an all-boys' Catholic school. It was a quiet and poignant moment, and I valued her being there. I appreciated the environment in which we talked about her past and my present; it was cooling in the fresh air, quite unlike other interviews I did which took place at home. I remember we did re-shoots of interviews in my own house, and it was stifling, as it was the middle of summer and we couldn't put the fan on. I don't know how it managed to turn out so well, and I was glad that I didn't sound like too much of an idiot. Pick-ups (reshoots) were also an amazing chance for me to see how much my voice had changed. In the title sequence, I did a voiceover after filming, which then switched to a shot of me speaking when I was only perhaps one month on T. The change in my voice is incredible for the little amount of time that had passed.

Towards the end of filming the documentary, I was taken shopping for some male clothes and also on a photo shoot just off Oxford Street with a professional photographer. We didn't end up buying any of the clothes (sadly) but Channel 4 used the shots that were taken by the professional photographer. I had a chance to show off my recently acquired tongue piercing, which was done sneakily one day in Camden. The shots were used everywhere; one is on the documentary's page on the Channel 4 40D website, others were used in the press – all very moody and alternative, with me posing in a black top hat and band T-shirt (yet to know if the band Finntroll have seen my subtle representation; I know other fans noticed). Some pictures were also taken with my mum, which was quite embarrassing as the strong studio lights and heat of the room made us sweat and it was sticky and clammy to have my face pressed up against hers. However we got some nice photographs taken together, all very cuddly and mushy (I prefer my solo ones with the top hat!) and as a present we got one blown up onto a huge piece of hardboard and given to us, as well as a nice black and white one for the mantelpiece. I suppose not many people have huge photographs of themselves hanging in their living room.

I finally got to see the film in a non-finished state when it was being edited in Cardiff, which was around

August. My tongue bar had fallen out after a drunken weekend camping and I hadn't bothered to replace it, though I now have it re-pierced with a septum piercing to add to my collection. I hadn't been to Wales before, I'd never needed to go, but it was a surprisingly short train journey up. I think from filming in dribs and drabs I had no idea what the finished product would be like, or even what bits would be used. I was excited to get a glimpse of the editing process for myself as I had always been interested in how films were made from religiously watching the appendices on the *Lord of the Rings* extended edition DVDs, and to radiate in being part of a successful film crew. I would also get to watch the finished cut for the first time before it went on air.

Nobody likes watching themselves on film, and I'm one of the worst people for it. I can barely watch other people say things to camera, I get embarrassed *for* them. I detested my voice back then; it was still in the stages of morphing into a deeper, fully broken voice, so I squeaked occasionally. The funniest thing for me to see was the inter-cutting between recently filmed clips and clips that were put together at the start of filming, back when I had long hair and a high voice. I remember the shot of me sitting on my futon in my pink room with long hair in a ponytail explaining how to rub in Testogel. My voice was near to how it was pre-T, and it's odd to think how one little sachet of gel every day for a few months can produce such drastic changes, as can be seen later on in the documentary when I have shorter hair. Apart from cringing at my breaking voice, I always thought I sounded too basic on film. I can never express myself how I want to. In my head I'm articulate but when words come out of my mouth they don't sound the same. But Julia and my mum and everyone else who'd seen the edits didn't seem to think that. And on the whole, I thought it was really good! I didn't sound *too* bad, not as bad as I thought I sounded in my head. It was funny in some places, with the right amount of my mother's story to show a different perspective on my transition, one that was fearful and speaking of loss. I didn't cry when I watched it, although others shed a few tears. It moved me, and I thought it was very informative. But I'm the sort of person who cries at fictional death scenes in *Harry Potter*; I'm not one to weep at the story of my own life. I felt awkward that I had found my story emotional, probably because I'm so used to making light of everything I go through. I made light of my self-harming and I made light of the severity of the bullying I was going through at school. I might cry to myself but never in public, never anywhere other people who believe I am strong can see me. My mum especially, it's always awkward for me to cry in front of her as I don't like to let my emotions affect her after all we've been through together. The last time I cried in front of her was probably the night I came out, a time of great emotion. Watching a documentary about myself didn't bring out any great emotions in me, because it was about things I knew already, and I didn't think they were enough to warrant tears.

I realised I haven't talked about how I came up with the name of the documentary. At the QYN meet, which was filmed but never shown, Julia asked a group of us for ideas on the title. We were packed into a Soho tea room, clustered together on benches and chairs, blocking out all other customers because there were so many of us. *The Boy Who Was Born a Girl* came up as a suggestion. At once there were moans of disapproval. No no no, far too problematic. This was my view as well; it was so, well, cheesy, for starters. Secondly, I was not 'born a girl', I was 'assigned female at birth'. But *The Boy Who Was Born a Girl* was left as the working title of the project, and I spectacularly failed to come up with a new one. It was OK – it sparked people's imaginations and made viewers want to watch it. I liked how they did the logo, with juxtaposing male and female symbols on each part, which the genderbender side of me liked.

Around the same time as the film editing I did an interview for the *Guardian*, the first press interview I did. My mum and I made a conscious decision to only give interviews to media we felt would present our story with integrity. The journalist from the *Guardian* had written about trans issues before – she was the author of the article that had inspired Julia to make a documentary. We also gave an interview for the *Lady* magazine, a strange choice, but again, a very good article was produced by a quirky and friendly young journalist. I turned down some women's mags, even though they offered money, and also turned down an offer to appear on one of the morning TV shows. I didn't feel comfortable being interviewed on live television. It's all OK when you have an editor to make you seem smart, and you have filmed hours upon hours of interviews with the best bits picked out, but I didn't trust myself to appear well informed on live TV, and I was also very self-conscious about my appearance. I was also worried that the hosts wouldn't understand me very well; and I had no idea what I would do if they asked odd or embarrassing questions.

The night the documentary was aired everyone in the house was in a state of anxiety. A few friends of mine were having a 'première' at one of their houses; my computer was on, ready to Facebook after the event. I don't know why I was so nervous. My mum, my ex-partner and I knew what to expect, and nothing spectacular would happen afterwards. But as the

Channel 4 voiceover guy introduced the programme, it was odd to think that *other people* would be seeing me. It felt strange, to know that right then I was being watched by other people. I had no idea of the reception it would get or whether, actually, a lot of people would watch it. There was a documentary about a parking attendant on beforehand, which we caught the end of, but we assumed that because of the title and the fact that it was on before *Big Brother* our documentary would pull a few viewers. We sat in silence as the title came up, and remained so for the next half hour, which seemed to crawl by. Then it was over. That, in twenty-five minutes, depicted months of my life and my first steps into transition. The emotions of the NHS, the private treatment and finally getting on testosterone; the months of filming, sitting and talking in front of a camera about being bullied, about school, about what transition means, what gender is: everything had been condensed down into half an hour. It was barely scraping the surface, but it was enough for people to see the human side to living life as a trans person.

I almost immediately rushed upstairs. I knew I would get some messages and I thought it would be nice to reply to a few of them. I logged on and immediately was greeted by a barrage of Facebook notifications. I sat down and stared at them incredulously. Damn, there were a lot of them. I started to reply to them, individually at first. Every single one of them was a positive comment, encouragement or feedback. I heard back from my friends who had been watching it at their house – they thought it was great, with the barber who cut my hair becoming a slight heartthrob online. I was pleased to know I'd done my friends proud, I respected their opinion of my expression of being a trans person. I was pleased I hadn't come across, at least to them, as too clueless and immature. I sat in front of my computer for hours. I was added as a friend by a flurry of people from my old school, and people who I didn't even know – I had *fans*. Strange but good: not quite the rock star's groupies I hope for in later life but a start!

This sort of attention and flattery wasn't something I was used to. Eventually I had to stop replying to messages individually. I just posted a couple of statuses on the Facebook page thanking people for their kind words. I felt, regardless of what any media reviews would say, that this had been a success. More than anything I felt a great sense of accomplishment for everyone involved, and was proud with how the project had turned out. I was overwhelmed too, that people thought this relatively low-budget documentary was so good. My words were heard by people and appreciated. I went to bed with a sense of relief that it hadn't gone horrifically badly.

Now I just had to wait for the proper aftermath. Aside from my well-wishers and friends on Facebook, I had to go back to the sixth form and face the reaction there. I had to come out to people who didn't know about my trans status before. I also had to face the community outside my house. Would I get recognised in the street? Would reviewers hate it completely, and would I be mocked in the press as just another young tranny sensation? The vile and cruel comments in the tabloids over the years about some of the younger girls at Mermaids still stung, and they had almost had their lives destroyed by prying journos. What if something similar happen to me? Only time would tell.

The next day the buzz hadn't died down. Messages of support still flashed up on my screen when I logged on to the computer. I didn't know how on earth people were finding me; I had changed my name on Facebook a while back, but it looked like the word about me had spread through friends of friends. I debated reading the comments left for me on the 4OD page. I shouldn't have worried really: around 99 per cent of them were very positive, full of praise for me and my mum. We were called brave. I was called mature – wise, even! I don't notice my own bravery. I guess it takes balls to come out as something still seen by many people as freakish, wrong and taboo, but I can't imagine doing anything differently.

The documentary actually ended up being re-aired a couple of months later, and was the highest viewed episode in the First Cut Channel 4 documentary series. It was also nominated for a Welsh TV award in the category of Best Documentary. We didn't win, but it was nice to think that a documentary on this subject was highly recognised as a good piece of filmmaking. I was pleased it worked for Julia, too; after her effort and encouragement and generally being a wonderful person, it was a relief that her first directing job had shone.

After the documentary we did get recognised, but not a lot, and my mum more so than me as I'd cut my hair again by the time the documentary aired. Testosterone had morphed my facial structure even deeper into masculinity. There was no negative recognition; everything was very positive, even around our local area. I got recognised within the trans community; in fact, I still do on occasion, which worries me – I don't still look like that, do I? In the month afterwards I received a few strange looks on the tube, but no one said anything. I still haven't been attacked – verbally or physically – for it, not even around some of the dodgier areas where I live, and not even at the sixth form.

Going back to the sixth form was surprising. I knew I couldn't remain very 'in' to the people who didn't know me previously at the sixth form. Even though it had been my choice to make the documentary, and

I knew I had to face the consequences of that, the school would tackle any further harassment or bullying I received because of it. I didn't really know what to expect, but I think at the back of my mind I had given up on the majority of the people there. From the support given to me by my friends and well-wishers online about the documentary (someone I didn't know even started a Facebook 'Like' page for me) I knew I had the strength to challenge anyone. It was a good documentary and it was informative. If people watched it and still didn't understand me, then there would be nothing else I could do. People's opinions had changed, people's understanding had broadened. I'd read that *The Boy Who Was Born a Girl* was being cited by medical and educational professionals as something to refer to when dealing with clients who were young and trans, and their families.

But the reaction at school mirrored everything I'd experienced so far. It was supportive. People who had not understood me previously began to see me as 'normal' almost; a normal guy. They hadn't known how I felt about the comments they made, or the extent of how I was feeling about school; that I felt I wasn't even human, just a freak show. Students in my year, who I didn't really talk to, had the courage to ask me about my transition. I hadn't had a chance to tell people that I was open to respectful questions. With the documentary behind me, I could have something to hold on to when explaining 'what I was'. I wasn't just relying on stuttered words and digging things out on the spot. I didn't really speak about it in school after that, only if I was asked, and usually that was by pupils in the lower years. I had fun playing with them when they asked what the documentary was about when they found out I had been in one. If I didn't want to explain what 'transgender' meant, I could simply say I was gay and watch their reaction with amusement. There were a few people who didn't move on from how they treated me before, but having now so much more respect at school, I didn't care about the minority. I had changed perceptions.

The documentary would begin to affect me in more personal ways. I noticed that in the following months, I started to see a lot of people commenting on its personal benefit to them. One person, who is now a friend of mine, only came out to himself and other people as transgender after seeing the documentary. I first met him shortly after he posted a comment on Facebook and he has transformed from a shy young person into someone who is now on hormones and has had surgery. Other people in the trans community have come up to me, even now, saying that I gave them the will and courage to come out. It's the best feeling about the documentary for me, and is one of the reasons why I am pleased to have done it. Not for personal gain, not for my own story to be recognised as just one singular instance of trans life, but to help other trans people realise that they are not an isolated case. That other people go through this same experience. The documentary also showed the world that we exist as individuals and also collectively. We are a strong minority. We deserve to be heard, and we deserve respect. When I hear stories of young trans people my age starting to come out to themselves and feeling confident in taking control of their identities and displaying them without shame, then that's when I feel the documentary has been a success.

The documentary was used as a reference for the latest (at time of writing) transgender young character in *Hollyoaks*. Portrayed sympathetically and empathetically by the actress and writers, it is a symbol of the slowly changing times. As more documentaries get made, the media taboo lessens and stereotypes are shown up for what they are. That is the reason why I wanted to do it.

I don't think the attention got too much for Mum and I to handle. It was the odd bit of recognition here and there, and I wasn't recognised at all in the streets of my town or in London. Reviews afterwards echoed the positive sentiments. In fact the only 'bad' one, and that wasn't even bad it was more blasé, was from the *Daily Mail*, and I was shocked that it wasn't slated more! They said the programme had done what the title suggested and that was that. Nothing even slightly transphobic!

The documentary has gone global and hopefully will be shown for years to come. It helped people the first time around, and is continuing to help people explain issues to friends and family, and maybe discover themselves. I would rather put myself out there for the benefit of other people than hide away because I am too annoyed at people asking me questions or talking to me. In fact, I'd talk to anyone who was interested in speaking to me after they saw the documentary. There's no reason for me to erase this from my life or to not talk about it ever again. Even though I may move on with my journey and transition, it's something I'm proud of. Nay-sayers have wondered what I'd do if I de-transitioned. I can't imagine that happening (although, yes, it is something that's happened to people), but I think I'd still be happy to talk about it, looking at it from a different viewpoint. It's been such a positive and fulfilling experience that I don't think I could ever be truly ashamed of the documentary, even if I did drastically alter my perception of my own gender.

As well as gaining an insight into film production, it's been a once-in-a-lifetime experience. I've been lucky, turning from being a fifteen-year-old with no hopes for transition to being a nineteen-year-old, looking back at something huge, something well-done. I'd never have believed it was possible. And maybe I don't give myself enough credit, maybe this is one of the things I do take lightly. From the reviews and the people touched by it – parents, young trans people, questioning people, older trans people – my mum and I have done a lot of good in the face of unknown and possibly severe consequences. The experience was part of me growing into myself as a person, allowing me to connect with people a lot more. I don't normally talk about my feelings. I might write them down, but I rarely give voice to them like I did. I think the experience of putting my feelings out there for all to see weakened the barrier between me and other people. I'm still a very closeted and quiet person, but I'm not afraid of speaking any more.

Many people have asked if we would ever make a follow-up documentary about our lives now. Maybe in the future. Actually, I think I'd like to make that a certainty!

Luisa: A documentary

In the summer of 2008 I came across an email on the Mermaids website. It was from a media production company, Green Bay. A producer was researching gender dysphoria and had made contact in the hope of speaking to parents with transgender children, which might then lead on to making a documentary. I decided to call, and had a long conversation with Julia, the *documentary filmmaker*. I told Jon about it that evening and he was really interested in the possibility of a documentary. I arranged to meet Julia and took Yvonne, a good friend, along for support and an objective viewpoint, so she could give me her honest advice after the meeting. I took a photo of Jon from a couple of years ago. It's a great photo of him on the sofa with his first cat, Christmas. I had treated him to bright red highlights, which he had wanted for ages. His shoulder-length hair had been blow-dried straight; he looks very androgynous.

I felt very comfortable with Julia at that first meeting; she was warm, easy to talk to and most importantly came across with great integrity. It was a good first meeting. The next step was to arrange for Jon and me to meet up with her. Jon really wanted to be part of making a documentary because it was so important for him to be able to tell others that being transgender did not make you a freak. He wanted a chance to show that he was just like other teenagers, with a love for music, clothes and socialising. The only difference between him and 'normal' teenagers was that growing up involved him embarking on a remarkable journey of transition because it was the only way that he could face a positive future and a life. Being transgender was not a choice he had made, it was a fact, and he had had to make a decision about how he was going to deal with that.

We told Julia that we would think about whether we would be prepared to take the next step forward and get back to her. I now know that she waited anxiously for our call. It had been around six months since her initial contact with Mermaids and there was a wall of silence from parents. That silence was totally justified and understandable as a documentary had been made some years back, and those involved had experienced distressing abuse, death threats and sensationalist intrusion from the media. Mermaids is cautious about any media coverage and protective of the confidentiality of parents and their transgender children. So the decision to go ahead was entirely ours. It was a difficult decision to make. Jon desperately wanted to do it and I wanted to hear the support from others. I wanted to hear that yes this was the right thing to do – go ahead and do it. But talking to friends, parents and people from Mermaids there was always a protective fear in their voices. I did not find the support I needed to hear. But the more doubt and fear I heard in people's voices, the more I realised that this documentary had to be made, and that it was right to make it.

So I made the decision to make the documentary with my son. It was an issue that had to be treated with the respect and understanding that it deserves. It had to be explained that in reality it affects about 100 British children and their families every year (statistic taken from *Guardian* article in 2009). It was a risk, a big risk. There would be consequences, some of which we could plan for and some that neither Jon nor I would be fully aware of till the documentary was aired. We were both prepared to deal with the consequences because it was so important to take this opportunity to show people the reality of a trans teenager embarking on the process of transition. I remember coming across a quote in a newspaper I was reading on the train into work. It said that our lives are sometimes defined by opportunities, even those that we choose to miss. We both made a choice not to miss this opportunity in our lives. There is no financial gain in making a documentary; being paid would compromise its integrity. Jon and I wanted to make this documentary because it needed to be made.

I was understandably cautious and put in place every proviso I could think of to protect Jon. Julia was 100 per cent supportive of this. We drew up a confidentiality agreement for the production crew to sign; there was to be no disclosure of surname, personal data or location to any third party. If there was, I had made sure that we would be in a position to sue Channel 4 and Green Bay. Jonathan was a minor and I was there to protect him. The production crew were fully on board, his welfare and mine were essential. We would go ahead on the understanding that we could pull out at any time and if we did, everything that they had filmed would be null and void. Even though I put everything I could think of into place to ensure our protection it was still a big decision, but we both knew it was the right one.

Preliminary filming began towards the end of 2008. The Head of Production at Channel 4 viewed the initial filming and approved that it go ahead. We would be filmed over a period of months and it would begin in earnest at the beginning of 2009. So in the New Year we took another step in our journey.

Jon's first day of returning to school as a boy after his Christmas break is where the official filming would begin. That night, his boy's uniform pressed for the morning, I made sure that Jon went to bed early. I kept myself busy pottering around down-stairs. I cleaned out the fridge, wiped down the kitchen surfaces and tidied up the living room – I needed distraction. It was getting late and I had to tire myself out for bed and sleep, but my mind was filled with anxiety, excitement, apprehension and worry for the next day. A bottle of wine later I called Julia in her hotel; she had said to call at any time if I needed to talk. She answered the phone and I could tell from her voice that she had been asleep for a while. I talked about my fears, my anxiety, that I was scared of the day ahead. I was not questioning our decision to make the documentary, I just hadn't expected to have the overwhelming feelings of anxiety that I did. We talked for an hour, Julia was calm, supportive and reassuring and, finally exhausted, I went to bed.

The next thing I heard was a loud rapping on the downstairs hall window and my name being called out. I jumped out of bed in a daze and legged it down the stairs, opened the door half asleep and there was the production crew with Julia waiting outside. It was 7 a.m., I had overslept! They were great; calming and positive as I dashed about like the proverbial blue-arsed fly! I looked rough, bags under the eyes, tracky bottoms and my baggy house jumper on. Filming began. Jon looked handsome in his boy's uniform, but he couldn't eat his breakfast as his hands kept shaking every time he tried to take a bite of toast. He was very nervous; it was a brave thing he was about to do. To go back to his school of around 2,000 students and be himself, the only transgender student there. He was just sixteen and his courage blew me away.

The time came to drop him off at school and we were running behind schedule. My car was frosted up and would not start. The production crew kindly gave us a lift to school, no filming took place here as one of the provisos was that neither the school nor any student would or could be involved in the documentary. I did not get out of the car, as Jon wanted to walk through the school gates on his own. I watched him through the back window as he went into school. What a brave and tremendous child, my son.

That morning we had agreed not to talk about how his day had gone till we got home and could be filmed. After I picked him up from school, we talked on camera, and it was important to capture the immediacy of our experiences on film. On camera Jon told me it had gone well, his close friends had been there to support him. There had also been the sadly expected verbal abuse and snide comments from other students, but he had got through that first day and I was relieved. I knew that it would be one day at a time from here on, some days would be OK and other days would be absolutely awful for him and that is exactly how it went. There would come a time when he could no longer take it and thankfully decided to tell me.

I arranged a meeting with the head of Year 11 about the harassment. I do not like confrontation at the best of times and have always tried hard in my life to be as reasonable as possible in times of difficulty and conflict. It seemed to be the younger students that were causing the problems. As the meeting progressed and I listened to what the head was saying, I felt myself grow angrier and angrier. She seemed to be telling me that some bullying was inevitable, that not much could be done unless there was tangible evidence, that they had already dealt with some of the bullies in line with school policy but unfortunately some instances could not be dealt with. I could feel the anger rising. I felt hot, slightly shaky, and then I spoke my mind. I did not raise my voice but I looked at my son sitting next to me and I thought, '*No bloody more of this beating around the bush.*' I was clear and direct in my message to her, I felt let down, outraged, hurt and very angry. I felt that my son was being let down.

My child had all the rights of any other child and his gender dysphoria did not take away these rights. He had the right to respect, he had the right to be individual, and he had the right to equal treatment. These rights were not questionable, we were not asking for any extraordinary treatment. We were just asking for what every parent would ask for their child: that they are treated well. Just as they had a duty of care to each and every one of their students, they had to fulfil their duty of care to my son. I felt fobbed off, having to battle and justify my son's rights. This battle is a significant part in the lives of many parents with transgender children, the constant wearing down of explaining to one professional or other why it is essential that your child gets treatment, counselling, support and understanding. It often takes you to a place of anger, but to make any progress you have to keep reasonable and focused in order to get the help and support needed. It really does wear you down and at times all that keeps you going is the love you have for your child, but it's worth fighting for. I knew school was never going to be easy, but I didn't reckon on exactly how hard it was going to be.

An initial meeting with the headmistress before Jon's return to school as a boy had gone well. She was supportive, caring and open about her lack of knowledge in this area; she had made contact with other heads that had experience of having a transgender student in their school. She reassured us that their duty of care was very important. What Jon and I really wanted was for the school to talk to students (with the permission of their parents) to give them an understanding of what it means to be transgender. I gave the school all the contact details of organisations that can help with educating staff and students on gender diversity: GIRES (Gender Identity Research and Education), Schools Out (they work towards equality in education for LGBTQ people), Gendered Intelligence (they provide creative and educational workshops within schools). The headmistress did not feel that this sort of education was necessary at that point in time and as a school they would handle informing the students they felt should be informed. I tried, but it was not going to happen the way Jon and I felt it should. We wanted the school to run a positive and informed campaign championing LBGTQ issues by those we felt had the right experience and knowledge to do so. I concentrated my energy and efforts on what I could do, which was to always be there supporting my child.

I told the school of our involvement in the documentary a couple of months after filming began. I did receive a call from the headmistress once the documentary was aired. It was shown on Friday 4 September 2009 and on Monday 7 September I got a call from the headmistress's secretary telling me to hold the line as the headmistress would like to talk to me. I could tell in her voice that it had made a profound impression on her. Jon's courage to be true to himself, the pain of the bullying, the love I have for my child. She said she had learnt so much from watching the documentary and it had given her an understanding of the difficulties that presented themselves. I was glad that our documentary had the positive impact we wanted, that had been the whole point. She now saw my son and the adversity that he was facing. I wished that she had seen this too before she watched the documentary.

Filming finished by the beginning of summer 2009 and Julia started the lengthy editing process. It had been an amazing experience and was a confirmation of my gut reaction that regardless of the huge step we were taking, it was the right thing to do. It had been emotional, it had made me feel vulnerable and raw at times, especially when I opened up and talked about my feelings of loss, the past and my memories, but it had also been therapeutic. Throughout, I never doubted the integrity of our documentary, and I knew that the message would be a positive one. Our final viewing after editing confirmed this. We had all worked towards the important messages of acceptance, understanding, integrity and love. We were all proud of the final achievement. Now we had to wait for it to be aired and the consequences.

The Boy Who Was Born a Girl
(Channel 4 – First Cut Series)

Sixteen-year-old Jon is your typical teenage boy in all respects except one – he was born a girl. Brought up as Natasha for fifteen years, Jon can remember feeling male since he was only five years old. He has now been diagnosed with gender dysphoria, a condition that affects over 100 British children every year, and is embarking on an extraordinary journey of transition. For his mother Luisa this means coming to terms with the enormous loss of her daughter, while supporting her son as he starts his hormone therapy treatment to become the man he's always known he is.

This First Cut film by Julia Moon follows mother and son through the first three months of Jon's life-changing treatment as the testosterone pushes his female body into male puberty. For Jon, the changes that follow are things he's always wanted, but his dramatic transition means that Luisa must acknowledge that her daughter has finally gone. The Boy Who Was Born a Girl is a positive, life-affirming film about one teenager's determination to be true to himself, and the extraordinary love and support of a mother.

Green Bay Media

As soon as the programme synopsis had been released to the media there was a great deal of interest. Our PR contact at Channel 4 told us which publications were interested in our story.

Jon and I made the decision to be extremely picky about which media coverage we might agree to, as what was paramount to us was the integrity of our documentary. We wanted nothing to take that away, so we turned down offers from magazines, tabloid press and TV appearances that would jeopardise that, because we strongly felt that a lot of the interest generated would become sensationalist and titillating. Our journey was the opposite of that. It felt good to have the courage to stand by that decision and turn down articles and interviews that we didn't feel were right, even if there was a substantial sum of money involved. After careful consideration, we gave one interview. It was with Viv Groskop from the *Guardian*. A friend had done an article with her a while back talking about her male-to-female transgender child, and she reassured us of Viv's professionalism and understanding of gender dysphoria. This was the only interview we did before the broadcast.

The night of the broadcast Jon, his partner at the time and I sat on the sofa, excited and anxious. We watched our documentary and when it had finished our phone rang constantly for the next hour and throughout the evening. Friends and family contacted us to say that it was moving and inspirational, that we had done the right thing to make it. I knew we had, it had to be done. It was a tremendous feeling of relief that it was so well received. Jon and I were proud of our achievement, of our decision.

Media reviews

The Boy Who Was Born a Girl is a quietly power-ful essay by producer/director Julia Moon about sweet and articulate sixteen-year-old Jon, who used to be a girl called Natasha. It's a genuinely lovely film, thanks to the honesty of both Jon and his mum Luisa. Jon is excited about his transforma-tion and Luisa is hugely supportive. But she has no hesitation in discussing her pain at the loss of her daughter Natasha. She says of her new son's excite-ment: 'His happiness is my grief.'

Radio Times

Sixteen-year-old Jon was born as Natasha, a pretty girl from London with a biological gender disorder that meant she should have been born a boy. Now taking testosterone tablets that make his voice drop and listening to heavy metal, Jon is getting rid of the person that he was while his mother feels she has lost her daughter, to be replaced by a male twin of sorts, and school, predictably, is a nightmare. Jon is blessed with a brilliantly understanding mother and a wisdom beyond his years, making this a moving and inspiring film.

Will Hodgkinson, *Guardian*

Julia Moon's film catches Jon at a moment of profound transition. Gender realignment issues aren't exactly unknown territory for TV documentaries, and they aren't always handled with the utmost sensitivity. But where Moon triumphs is in her communication of the emotional nuances of the process, for both Jon and his mother Luisa. Typical of this is a wonderful scene in which the pair are refreshing Jon's wardrobe. Jon's embarrassed by the bras and dresses. His mother's proud, but fighting back tears. She's gained a son, but lost a daughter. It's a notable achievement to pack such depth into such a short film, but it's a feat that is increasingly typical of this fine series. Highly Recommended.

Time Out

As for the *Daily Mail* review, we had turned down the paper for a pre-broadcast interview article, so we felt that we had been given what we now refer to as the Ronseal Review. Ronseal is a trademark range of varnishes and paints. Its TV adverts have the tag line – 'It does what it says on the tin!'

So the *Mail* seemed to be suggesting that this documentary was as expected and nothing to write home about. It seemed a very dismissive statement and so we gave it a nickname!

The documentary was watched by over a million

people and outperformed the First Cut series and slot averages.

Posts that were left on the Channel 4 board and other websites

We expected there would be negative comments and inevitably there were. In general they expressed that:

Jon was far too young to make this sort of decision. It was not a reasoned one.

It was inevitable that he would realise his mistake and wish to change back to a girl.

He was selfish and thoughtless to put me through this.

He was not born male and therefore could never, would never be one. As his assigned sex was female at birth, tampering with it made no difference.

However, all the positive comments outweighed the negative ones.

Parents who had children with gender dysphoria spoke of their journeys, how they were touched and inspired by our integrity to share our story so publicly. How our documentary mirrored some of the difficulties in their lives.

Parents who did not have children with gender identity issues left other words of support. There were those that said they had never left messages on a post board before but after seeing our documentary felt it was important to do so and express how extraordinary and remarkable we both were. I must say in all honesty that it was wonderful to hear the words 'extraordinary' and 'remarkable' but it was also difficult to accept. We had embarked on making the documentary not because we felt extraordinary or remarkable but because we both just wanted to show that here was a family unit, a mother and child, two people that were living their lives. What was essential to us both was to show that unexpected as things may be, they are not as extraordinary as life presents them. To make them a part of our everyday living, a positive part, is what life is truly about.

Young people, adults beginning transition, those who were already well into their lives of transition, spoke of the positive impact it made on them. And for those who were struggling it gave them a hope that they could live their lives as the individuals they were meant to be and that there can always be a positive future.

Some people just left messages to affirm how remarkable and diverse life is and how important it was to them to see this being reaffirmed and essential to have the will and belief in achieving what you want to be in life.

The documentary was also nominated for a Bafta Award in the category for Best Factual Programme 2009.

I was so proud of my child. What was overwhelming and very unexpected for me, and still is, was the extraordinary reaction as to how amazing I was as a mother. It is humbling. I am just a mother, and loving your child is what it means to be a mother. Loving your child without conditions; it is just as simple as that. I cannot understand otherwise. So to read comments that were left about my tremendous motherhood made me feel sad, proud and uncomfortable. Sad because others did not have the support and love that they deserved. Proud because of the courage my son was being recognised and respected for. Uncomfortable because I do not feel that I am extraordinary, I am just being the mother that I have to be. There is nothing extraordinary about loving your child. It is extraordinary not to love.

The day after the documentary was broadcast Jon and I were shopping in the local supermarket. A woman approached us and said that she was sorry to interrupt us but had seen our documentary and wanted to tell us both that we were brave and it had meant a lot to her. That was our first reaction from a total stranger. A few months later I was at a meeting in London for the Annual LGBT Consortium and during the lunch break a young man came up to me. He apologised for intruding but asked if he could talk to me. He told me that he had watched the documentary with his girlfriend and thanked me for having the courage to make it. His social worker had watched it too; this young man was transgender and had been trying for years to convince the adoption authorities that he and his girlfriend should be eligible to adopt. His social worker had been supportive but the constant questioning, investigations and lack of progress was wearing everybody down. The authorities were not sure whether it was appropriate for a transgender to adopt, even though he was in a happy and secure relationship. He told me that thanks to the documentary there had been the most profound changes in their lives over the last few months. Their social worker now had a very different understanding; she fought their corner with a conviction and acceptance of the truth. They had finally been approved and would be adopting twins within the next couple of months. He thanked me again and said it was a direct outcome of our documentary. I was very humbled and touched that such a positive change had been made in this couple's lives and it had been because of us. I never found out if this couple's adoption was successful but I would like to think that they are now a family unit.

There were many voices that expressed the impact, in one way or another, that our documentary had made to their lives. Jon and I had done what we so wanted to do and we had achieved beyond what we thought we would.

Medical professionals, university lecturers and counsellors contacted Green Bay to get copies of the documentary. It is now used to educate, inform and give a better understanding of gender dysphoria. It has been distributed on an international basis and continues to touch the lives of others. Against all odds, my son Jon and I have left a mark on this world, we have made a difference, we have dared to be what we needed to be and are the better for it. It is my privilege to know and have this son.

Eight
Medical Transition

Jon: Becoming Jon

One of the things most commonly associated with the transition of a transgender person is the medical side of things, when they stop being a 'transgender' person and become a 'transsexual' (a term commonly used to describe a transgender person who has undergone medical procedures to match their internal sense of gender to their outwardly perceived sex). Not all trans people choose to undergo this, many are happy with their bodies and don't feel the need to modify them. Some will only want partial transition, such as surgery or hormones, and some cannot undertake medical transition.

I am a firm believer that your sex is whatever you

say it is. Your body is *yours*, and as a consequence you should label as you see fit; your genitalia is yours to call whatever names you please. Just because I was assigned female at birth does not mean I have to label my sex as female. My sexual identity is firmly male, and I refer to specific parts of my body as male. Also, with my medical treatment (hormones) my body and genitals do not look stereotypically female any more. I enjoy looking at my body in the mirror. It's an odd, but intriguing sight. The masculine shape, the fat distribution squared off and the curves pared down, but still with the undertones of big hips and defined waist. The breasts are still there, but morphed into semi-manboobs, with a wider, flatter cleavage, but with firm breast tissue supporting them. I'm covered in hair everywhere (a genetic trait from the Mediterranean side of my family, where *everyone* seems to be hairy). I now consider myself to have a penis, whether or not it would be described as such by others.

I wanted to go on hormones from the outset. I had a firm desire to change my perceived sex to male, to fit the sex I identified with. The term 'gender reassignment surgery' really gets me. There's no gender to be 'reassigned' – the gender is firmly in place inside the person! I always hated being perceived as female before testosterone. That's the simple reason why I wanted to go on it – the dysphoria at being taken always as a cis woman. It's hard to describe the disassociation you have with your body as a trans person. It's an estrangement. It's an extra piece of baggage hindering you from living your life. Some trans people may see it as a deformity, a birth defect, which is understandable and, for them, true. They were not meant to be born like that. I don't see it as a birth defect – I see it as an unfortunate event, but one that I accept. However, my body before testosterone, where I viewed my sex as female, has no relevance to anything I am now. I was not 'female-bodied', I suppose, even when I was presenting as one and mentally identifying as one. I always viewed my sex as something different – I always knew there were aspects to how I viewed my body, underneath it all, that were different from how other girls viewed theirs. Until I learned more about gender and sexual identity, I didn't know that you could make a seemingly female-sexed person transform into who I always imagined myself to be.

Before starting testosterone I had a firm image of exactly who I wanted to be. This was a combination of figures and types that I had always looked up to. I wanted a beard, badly. I loved beards, stemming from my obsession with *Lord of the Rings*. I'd *always* wanted one. Nowadays, I go clean-shaven – that just shows you how your body perception changes once you're on T. I wanted long hair, too, to emulate my metal heroes. I'd always imagined myself as a guy with long hair, perfect for headbanging. Before testosterone, having long hair wasn't possible – someone who appeared androgynous-ish, with long hair, is often taken as female. And with long hair, I often was. On testosterone, I need not worry about that. I could have extremely long hair, and people would still take me as male.

The man inside my mind was me, no matter what he looked like: a clean-shaven, androgynous-yet-male goth-rocker, a long-haired, bearded warrior: these were all me. *This* was my body, not the frame I had been born with. After I learned about taking ownership of my gender, and not being afraid to come out about it, I started to feel unafraid of talking about how I wanted to match my gender to my physical shape. I wanted to become the man I had always dreamed of being. And I knew this wasn't a lie or child's fantasy or role play gone too far. How do you know you're a man? How do you know you're a woman? You just do, intrinsically. And I knew intrinsically who I was, without outside influence. I identified with certain things without anyone telling me to. I knew that my exterior was false. During the end of my stay at the Bethlem psych ward, I realised that that I could change this exterior that was holding me back from being who I was. There were options for me; there were options to remove the baggage of being perceived as female.

I knew none of these options (the different types of surgery, the different hormones) could be entered into lightly, and I definitely wasn't going to jump into anything I didn't know about. But I knew what I wanted the end result to look like. I had to be on testosterone; there was no way I could just live with the constant ambiguity, the constant 'threat' of looking like a butch female, someone I was not. There are different courses for different people, and I knew which one was right for me, even at fifteen. Some people may think at that age I was far too young to be making my own choices, but I knew better than anybody who I was, and no one would be able to tell me otherwise! Confusion? A phase? Well, if it's a phase it's been going on for a very long time! And even then, I was sure. Talking to other trans people, learning about their experiences and talking to them about how I perceived my gender, I was sure that it wasn't a phase I was going through. But if it had turned out as such, it would be my own mistake, and no one would be to blame apart from me.

All I knew at this point was the hopelessness of not being able to secure a male sex. The hopelessness of thinking about how I would look and sound in the future, and being disappointed it wouldn't be me; that

I would always be a dreamer. The exercise of 'imagine if you woke up in the body of the opposite sex' doesn't help to empathise with what a trans person feels like. Imagine being stuck in that body for years, without the chance of changing, and having to deal with that every day, from morning until evening. It's more than waking up and looking in the mirror. There's navigating jobs, and relationships, and the world. Simply saying, 'It's what's inside that counts' is irrelevant to many trans people, and it is to me. We project images of ourselves into the world. If you are a man inside but the world sees a woman on the outside, you're not going to work in society. You can't work. You will feel inadequate and like a liar and hopeless. You want to, you *need* to change. Maybe by aspiring to ideals and dreams of who you are inside, like I did, or seeking a path forward and rolling with the changes, as I learned to do once on testosterone. The fact is that transitioning is vital for a person to live. As transgender is believed by some to be an illness, then talking about and exploring gender variance, and perhaps transition into your true self, is the only viable cure.

I first began thinking about what options I would go for in 2008, when I was sixteen. By talking to friends who were already starting to transition, and who knew a lot more about transition than I did at that age, I began to explore the options I was presented with. I was transitioning socially just fine, with Mum's help. Social transition (living full-time as your gender) is the be-all requirement for receiving any form of treatment on the NHS. The other requirements are being over eighteen. I began by dressing in male clothes full-time, referring to myself as Jonathan and 'he', which was made easier now that I was out around my mum. She's admitted it did take her a while to get used to 'he'ing me, and that it was a while before the name 'Natasha' stopped popping into her head. That was understandable: for fifteen years of my life I had been her Natasha, and now she had to get to know a new name for her child. It must have been hard. But I am impressed and surprised that she's never birth-named me or 'she'd' me a lot in the early stages after I came out to her and began living as male. I remember the first time she bought me male clothes, for my birthday that year. It was a pair of striped skinny jeans from the guy's section, and a Batman Joker T-shirt. She said it felt odd, but good at the same time. I was over the moon that she had my guy clothing choices down to a T (whenever she buys me a T-shirt or a pair of shorts on a whim, she always gets it right, I guess it's that mother–son connection!).

After presenting myself full-time as male for around half a year or more, and discussing options and modes of transition with other young trans people, it seemed like the next step would be to go to the NHS, to get hormones and surgery. At that time I was binding my chest every day. A binder is like a compression vest used to flatten the chest and make it appear more masculine. The feeling of binding is reminiscent of wearing a corset made out of semi-stretchy material, like a plastic bandage vest, and it comes with all of the perks of a corset. Your breasts are squashed up against you, and sometimes, in spite of your efforts to flatten them, make a 'speed bump' underneath your shirt, which means yet more layering of clothing. As I only have a B cup I have been spared the pain of binding larger breasts. But still, binding did give me discomfort for the time that I did it. Summer especially, as because you don't have a socially acceptable male chest you're not allowed to strip off, and have to continue sweating under a heavy vest.

I don't think many people appreciate the severe health risks associated with binding. Many people think that it's just like a tight vest. But the health problems associated with binders can be considerable: bone and muscle problems in the back and chest are common, as well as breathing difficulty and severe discomfort. One of my friends has had to undergo surgery from years of binding, another has had fluid build up in the brain because of the tightness. It was documented in *Dad's Having a Baby* that one of the trans men had to have a nipple removed after catching gangrene through open sores created by binding. Fortunately, I've only ever had muscular ache; I think I've been very lucky, and no doubt it would be worse if I continued to bind now. I have only stopped because the combination of a year and a bit worth of binding, plus years on testosterone, make the breasts sag, and so I have no real need to hide them even in a T-shirt in summer! Binding now would be maximum effort for minimal results. I would have to spend a good five minutes trying to contort my body into it!

In early transition I had severe dysphoria with my chest and sometimes it still irks me, although it is nowhere near as bad as before. I remember one night I wasn't able to touch my body because of the pain I felt when I did. I lay there at night not wanting to acknowledge I had breasts or any other gendered parts. I remember I just wanted to be a head, without a body to exist, without these parts that burdened me. Sometimes I still look in the mirror, debating whether I should pay to have surgery now. Wondering if I could go another summer without being shirtless and comfortable. Sometimes I wonder if I should just not care what anyone else thinks, and bare my chest anyway, proud of my difference. But as much as I feel apathetic towards my chest now, with the changes it has undergone, I can't help thinking that it is still a burden. It's noticeable that I don't bind, and it's still there for people to look at and question. Not that I mind people questioning, a bit of gender bender is a good thing, but if I were to relax in the park shirtless my chest would be viewed as strange. It wouldn't be acceptable, even though I would have a male every-thing else from the looks of it. All I would have is a bit of surplus breast tissue.

In 2008, I went to my GP, who was kind enough to send off a prompt referral to the Tavistock Clinic. At that point I just wanted hormones as quickly as pos-sible. I didn't mind too badly about binding but I was petrified of not being taken seriously by anyone when I started in the sixth form, or having to go to a new college as weird and ambiguous, not passing and having to explain myself over and over again. I longed for the freedom of expression that testosterone would give me. It would give me the changes I needed to be the man I wanted to be. In short, I wanted to get my future started as quickly as possible. I was sure of myself: I knew the risks, side effects and proce-dures from researching them online and talking to friends. I knew what types of testosterone treatment there were, what each of them provided and how long each change would take. I'd had some counselling beforehand, as this is a required part of undergoing transition, and my counsellor had said that I was ready to receive treatment. Being only fifteen, there's the capacity for medical professionals to spin things out. Many of my friends have had this, and it's common to experience endless waiting lists and vague appointments with the gender clinic doctors, who seem to want to delay a determined young person's transition for as long as possible. It's a sickening procedure, and after that first Tavistock Clinic appointment I came out with a feeling of dread. I was facing rigorous probing about my childhood – which toys I played with, family history, etc. – and I got the feeling that my previous history of depression would count against me and make the doctors be extremely wary of proceeding with treatment, even though I wasn't even considering gender identity when I was depressed. While writing this I have looked at a friend's social networking page. He is one of my trans inspirations, talking to him about trans issues has helped me shape and feel more confident in my own identity. He's just posted an update. 'Jesus,' it says, 'it's taken me four years to get on T.' This man is one of the smartest and clued-up people about trans issues I have ever met, and he is well over eighteen. He went through the NHS, and it took him four years to receive treatment and start feeling comfortable again, to start living. It's shocking and upsetting to think this is the current situation for many trans people, who haven't got the means to go private. These are long years, which they have no control over, ending up with a lot of people suffering from depression, body hate and self-loathing. I don't think I could have waited that long. I can't even imagine waiting that long to begin life again, to be taken seriously, to stop loathing the sight of myself and to stop justifying myself to everyone else.

I went private in early 2009. I realised that I, like many other young trans people, would not be listened to, and would have to deal with the farce of being under the age of eighteen and starting transition without the help hormone treatment. Since I went privately, a lot of other young people who had started out with me on the NHS, have also made the same decision. It was a lot of money for Mum to afford at the time, about £200 per session, however, in the long run, Mum and I knew it was our only option. From the reports we'd heard, it might only take a few sessions to get started on treatment (if you were deemed ready enough to begin testosterone).

I went to my first appointment soon after I had been to the Tavistock Clinic. Dr Curtis was at that time the only private gender identity doctor in London (in the UK, I think), and 'going Curtis' was seen as the norm when one felt let down and angry at the system. I had heard good reports about him, and had heard that he took young people seriously. My first assessment would be based on my recent mental health and my feelings about my gender identity, and to see if anything could conflict with that. All in all, on the day when I exited Bond Street tube station, I was feeling all right with it all. I believed nothing could be as disheartening as the experience I had had at the Tavistock Clinic.

The clinic is up in an office on Harley Street, sur-rounded by nice-looking private dental practices and cafés that sell expensive coffee. You press a buzzer reading 'Dr Richard Curtis' among many Arabic and Indian names. You take the lift up and enter the waiting room, which looks more like someone's living room, rather than an actual clinic: there is a sofa and some chairs, and a carpet, and a very homely looking desk piled with papers, a large green house plant to one side, magazines on the tables, even a small library of transgender-themed reading, and little notices about support groups on the walls.

I was greeted, at my first appointment, by a polite secretary, who was well liked by all the transgender people I knew who had been through the clinic. I took a seat, and reached for a magazine, feeling incredibly at ease. I heard behind me the sound of the laser clinic and my mum and I winced, knowing the procedure going on inside – a hair removal session – was most likely extremely painful. It really did sound like tiny electric shocks going off sporadically every few seconds, which stood out in the comforting, padded silence.

We had the good fortune of arriving on time, and ten minutes after Mum and I had arrived, we were called into Dr Curtis's office. I took a seat opposite Curtis, in a wide, comfortable chair, while my mum sat at the back of the room on a sofa.

Dr Curtis was pleasant to me, and I had no problems in talking to him about what I wanted, why I had left the NHS route, and what I expected in my transition. I knew what questions to expect, and what answers to give, a trick one has to learn if one is going through the Charing Cross GIC or Tavistock mode of transition. But I felt relaxed in giving my answers and I didn't feel the need to play up my masculinity. I suppose the fact that Curtis is also trans helped a lot. We instantly had that experience in common. I didn't feel he had any privilege over me, and wasn't 'gatekeeping'.

It was in either the second or third session that we talked about what form of testosterone I would take. He deemed me ready enough for testosterone treatment at that appointment, and I left his offices with a weight off my chest: I was going to get the process under way sooner rather than later. This process had taken years off my transition, something that I continue to be grateful for. I have a suspicion that even now, over two years down the line, I would only just be starting to access treatment, rather than being over two years past my start date.

So after I'd had a blood test that would deem me medically fit enough to take testosterone (I was, but was advised that I should stop smoking and start exercising, two things I've never been able to get the hang of), Curtis held up a chart of all the different forms of testosterone, and how bad each would make my mood swing. He explained to me that gel would be the one he recommended, as it was more controlled than an injectable dose of testosterone, which gave the user a strong rush, which tapered out towards the end. There are two common forms of injectable solution in the UK, Nebido and Sustanon 250. Less common are implants and patches, which I think are more popular in the US. Gel could be applied every day, and was likely to not have as severe side effects as the other forms. I agreed with Dr Curtis, and started off on gel, which I was able to get prescribed through my GP on the PCT (Primary Care Trust) – if not, it would be around £50 a box, which lasted a month. I would start off on gel, to get my body used to it. In any case, I didn't like the sound of the side effects of the injections: dips and troughs in mood, anger, and strong emotional flares, which was one of the things my mum was concerned about – me, changing before her eyes, into a 'wild child' on T, no longer the shy and quiet girl she once knew.

I started applying one sachet of Testogel every day, beginning in April 2009. I knew that the changes I should expect were to be gradual, but consistent. I knew some trans guys who had switched to injections soon after starting on the gel, being unhappy at the progress. I, however, experienced some immediate effects.

The increase in hunger was the most noticeable thing. I was always hungry, a shift in the attitude I had towards food. Before, I could eat small portions and snack often, but on testosterone, I ate much, much more. Even after two years, I'll eat anything, and lots of it. I remember the first Christmas after starting testosterone. Instead of having one serving of the Christmas roast, I had three large helpings and pudding for afterwards, plus sweets and chocolate. I think that was pretty good going!

I immediately felt a kick, a rush, the first night that I applied the gel. T is a powerful drug, and even now that my body's had two years to get used to it, I still get a rush after a few days of it being injected into me. Testosterone, like all drugs, affects different guys in different ways. In my case, I was happy at the rate of transition and, unlike other guys I knew, I wasn't sensitive to it. I could lather on a sachet a day with ease, and when I forgot I usually did two to compensate, with no side effects whatsoever – no shakes or mood swings. I don't think I got many of the strong effects some people report: there was no insatiable lust or anger. Actually, I think I've become less angry in that I've internalised anger more, and I have become more rational in arguing with people, rather than just shouting at them. I didn't experience any real emotional swings; although now I'm having injections, I have noticed an increase in my depression towards the end of the hormone cycle every three months, when the testosterone peters away and the oestrogen starts to come back.

To my and Mum's relief, I was still Jon as I was pre-T, but with changing facial features. My mum has also said I've become more confident on testosterone, but I don't think this is an effect of the T itself; I've just become more confident in how I present myself and my appearance.

For the first time, I was proud of my face and of my body. Metamorphing in front of the mirror was a man, slowly starting to emerge from his shell, and he wasn't half bad-looking either! Day by day went past and I saw my first subtle changes in facial shape: my jawline becoming more defined, straight and chiselled, a definitely male, yet elegant jaw. My face gradually 'melting', as I put it; the fat redistributing as Dr Curtis said it would, making my features more angular and rugged than smooth and feminine. I was growing my hair long at the time – in the beginning I had it tied back into a ponytail, then it was wavy and mid-length, just above shoulder height. I cut it shorter when I began to pass as male, shaving it into a faux hawk and spiking it up with gel. Listening to the takes from the documentary, it was startling to see how much my voice was beginning to change. It was clear I had a female voice in the beginning; even if it was the lower end of the register, like my mother's, it was definitely female. After a few months it started gradually to break. Not noticeably, never so much that I squeaked or quavered and people would comment on it, perhaps once here or there. I never noticed it deepen though; you don't notice how your voice sounds until you hear it back. My voice has always sounded the same in my head, apart from those strange times where you hear what you actually sound like. It must have been strange for the viewers; I wonder how much it did change overnight, or over the course of a few weeks or months. Now, I think my voice has pretty much stopped changing, and I can't do a female voice if I try, I just sound very camp. Some trans guys, who maybe hadn't had lower-register voices pre-T, have a slight camp lilt to their voice, something I had noticed when I was around trans people, but something I didn't really mind if it happened to me. I think, however, that I am quite average-voiced, although I'm naturally camp anyway. I hesitate to say that I have a low voice, in my head it's quite low, and I dance around the house with my headphones in, blasting out operatic baritones that I never thought I could ever reach. I probably sound much less impressive than I do in my head.

Some people report that their sexuality changes on testosterone. While this may be a combination of various factors, it does seem to happen quite a lot – previously straight identified men will 'turn gay'. I believe that this is more to do with the fact that you are feeling more at ease with yourself, and more confident in getting a partner, whereas before you may have had to fill the queer/lesbian stereotype to get any queer-understanding partner. As your moods change your perceptions of things start to change, so may your perception of who you find attractive. Personally, nothing changed sexuality-wise, for me; I've always been fluid, but I started to be more comfortable in admitting I found men more attractive than women; I felt that now I didn't need to present as a gay woman, I could be who I was: a queer man. A friend of mine was straight for all the time I'd known him pre-T. I met up with him a few months ago, and he'd said everything had changed! I was very surprised, but it made sense: another one that had been 'turned', we joked. I personally know more queer trans men than straight ones; something some medical professionals find puzzling, but I think it makes sense. In many ways, the transgender and queer communities are interlinked, and a transgender person would be exposed to more sexual identities and concepts of fluid sexuality and gender identity. I find watching previously straight-identified people turn queerer and queerer amusing; I like the fact that as trans people they don't feel the need to conform to expectations of a cis-centric and heteronormative society, and feel that they are free to express their sexualities as non-conforming to typical trans stereotypes.

One of the biggest changes that T would bring to me that I was looking forward to was facial hair. My genetics meant that I was always naturally hairy, especially in terms of leg hair, so I expected that I would grow facial hair pretty quickly – many other guys remain peach-fuzzed for years. I started to experience the darkening and thickening of my facial hair a few months in, and I was beginning to grow a small goatee and moustache, not wiry bristles, but the hair, while soft, was thick and black. After persevering, I managed, about a year on, to grow quite an impressive goatee, with two forked bits at the end. I couldn't grow it very long; I kept cutting it as the ends got thin and stringy; but it was a proper beard nonetheless! For aesthetic reasons I had always craved a beard. It just meshed with my personality so well: I was the geeky goateed metalhead boy or the gothic gentleman or the indie scruff. The beard and the sides and the sideburns could all be played around with; and I could easily transform from an everyday Primark jeans-and-T-shirt guy into a surly rocker. I didn't find it at all itchy to grow, only after shaving it or trimming it and re-growing it did I find it itchy, but after that, nothing. I enjoyed twiddling with it and pulling it, and I loved that it made me look older, so much older than many of the other guys on T who, due to their still boyish faces, got mistaken for young teenagers. My beard was a lifesaver when I went out to pubs, and if I had been a little taller than my short frame then I'm sure I wouldn't have ever needed to worry about underage ID. (Something that the T didn't do was give me a growth spurt, neither in height nor in foot size.) But you may notice that I am referring to my beard in the past tense. I have since gone for a different look and am shaven much of the time. Granted, when I do, it does make me look younger, but you need to switch up your style once in a while. I didn't think I'd ever like a clean-shaven look, but I'm thinking I'm starting to prefer it to my bearded face. I get stubble, proper stubble, every two days, and I need to shave (if I can be bothered) every three to four days.

My periods took a while to stop, a few months at least, longer than many other trans guy on hormones I'd known, but I didn't mind it that much since they weren't affecting me a big deal, and were more of a nuisance. They weren't heavy, and didn't last for long. I was asked by Dr Curtis if I wanted to freeze my eggs: testosterone can affect fertility, and even though some men do regain use of their wombs after stopping testosterone, if they want to have a child, there's no certainty. I did not take this procedure; it's expensive and I've never wanted biological children. I know this may be too early to say, but I've always thought of adoption. I'm not keen at all on the idea of birth!

I started physically passing more a few months in, even before my voice had started to fully break. I think people, especially family and friends, using my correct male name and male pronouns made this easier, and I also presented typically like a teenage guy; I was now comfortable in the way I dressed. I never tried to out-butch myself and relaxed my presentation into something everyday and fitting my personality. There wasn't a specific point where I started to pass 100 per cent; it gradually grew, steadily, like the changes I was undergoing. But I think it's safe to say that a few months in on T, I was starting to find passing easier.

The gel form of testosterone, for me, became a nuisance and is one of the reasons why I switched to Nebido, an injectable form of testosterone. I tend to forget to take any medication I'm on, and having scheduled injections every three months was much better for me in the long term, albeit quite a painful solution. Gel also smells like hospital, and takes a long time to dry. There is far more gel in one sachet than you realise, and you end up running out of body space to rub it on, and have to stand in your underwear for about half an hour to let it dry. Although some say Nebido gives quicker reactions and is more intense in the rush than gel, I've not seen any real difference. There is a buzz of well-being shortly after the shot, but I haven't experienced any real ups or downs to a great extent, nor an increased pace of physical changes. However, this works for me, and everyone needs to choose which form suits them best. For someone with a bad memory, scheduled appointments are definitely the best thing for me.

Luisa: Tell me about the dinosaurs

When Natasha told me that she was a boy, I focused on getting help and treatment for my child. Natasha was already in counselling for her depression with the local Child and Adolescent Mental Health Service

(CAMHS). She had been referred by our GP and we had been lucky because her counsellor was excellent. A friend of mine had been with the same service provider for a couple of years; her daughter, who had a different condition to Nat's, had been referred there too and she was constantly having to battle with counsellors and medical professionals to get the necessary treatment for her child. This, I would come to realise later, was a recurring theme in the medical profession: it's very hit and miss as to the timescale and quality of care that you get. It was dependent on the person you landed with as a professional. We were lucky, but I have too often heard of the endless frustration, tears and distress caused to families who are emotionally vulnerable and desperately in need of positive care and support. You are already worn down by dealing with the situation you are in and to add to this you then have to fight your way through red tape and poor professional advice.

It took Natasha a while to open up in counselling (her sessions with the counsellor were one to one, I was only involved if he had any pressing concerns for her personal safety). It was a relief that she was getting help even though her progress felt slow at times. She did not disclose her 'secret' to me or the counsellor at that point.

Once her secret was 'out', those initial first days

and weeks merged into a feeling of confusion and a sense of loss and losing oneself. Which way to turn? Who could help? What treatment was there? Where would she be referred to? How long did it take for referrals? What were the steps involved in the process? What exactly was transgender? How did it happen? What support was there? Were there other mothers feeling like me? How about other fifteen-year-olds feeling like my child? The only sure thing I did know was that I had a lot to learn and that the single most important thing right now was to get the help that my child needed.

So I began, googling and trawling through websites during my breaks at work, reading, gathering information. Trying to understand terminology, avoiding long scientific articles that felt like too much jargon for my tired and overloaded brain cells! I kept it simple, reading publications on gender dysphoria, ranging from concise NHS documents to posts and information on transgender and LGBTQ websites. There was a great deal of information out there but when you feel raw and confused it is difficult to take a lot of objective information on board, so I tried to take it in a little at a time. Nat did not really talk about her feelings of gender dysphoria and I did not press her. I was still trying to make sense of my feelings.

With Nat's consent, I called her counsellor, only to be informed that he was away on holiday and would not be back for a week. I left a long garbled message on his voicemail and made an appointment to take Nat to our GP. I kept a watchful eye on her and reassured her of my love every day. I didn't talk to anyone about it. Her counsellor called on his return to the office, I remember I was at work and took the call outside on my mobile. I did a lot of not getting to the point, finding it difficult to tell him what my child had told me the night she came out. When I did, it was unexpected news to him. Nat had not talked about her feelings of gender dysphoria at any of their counselling sessions. We had a long chat and arranged her next session. I always spoke to Nat before doing anything on her behalf. Honesty and communication is important in this life. It has kept our bond strong during difficult times.

Our GP was totally supportive; he had some knowledge of gender dysphoria although he had not dealt with a patient my daughter's age. He said he would liaise with CAMHS and deal with the refer-ral to the Tavistock Clinic (Tavi) and their Gender Identity Service. In the meanwhile it was a case of waiting, we knew it was going to take time. This was confirmed by the stories and progress (or lack of) made by other parents with transgender children.

At our end, the GP and counsellor were very aware of the time factor being important for Nat's emotional and mental well-being and they were expedient with paperwork, funding queries and getting the referral placed, and they both took the time to sort out the 'letter loop' from the Tavistock end. Here is an abbreviated version of how part of that loop went: the Tavi sent a letter to CAMHS asking for their initial referral from the GP, CAMHS sent this, then another letter was requested from the GP to confirm this (although the GP had already confirmed this in his first letter to them). Back to the GP regarding NHS funding, GP reiterates that CAMHS are the ones dealing with funding and they are fully aware of this. Letter to CAMHS from Tavi regarding funding. Letter from CAMHS to Tavi confirming funding. Letter to CAMHS and GP from Tavi to confirm letters received regarding funding.

Eventually the letter loop came to an end and one great day we received Nat's first appointment letter. It had only taken about three months and I mean only, because good fortune seemed to be on our side! The waiting list for an initial appointment can be up to six months and more. It felt like a big step forward. We would both soon learn that it was a very small step towards any possible treatment.

I heard mixed reviews about the Tavistock. Some parents, children and teenagers felt very let down by them. Waiting lists were long and getting longer. On a positive note, I met others who had received good professional support and help and were confident in the treatment plans provided. Nat and I went with an open mind, hoping for the best.

By our third meeting with the psychotherapist, the hope had gone. The previous two sessions had concentrated on Nat's childhood, which is all well and good and obviously needs discussion in relation to her gender identity. The therapist talked about Nat's memories of play. Jon was honest and intelligent and had a good sense of humour during these sessions, but we both came out feeling frustrated at the lack of timescale towards a treatment plan or even discussion of possible treatment. Many parents have expressed similar feelings, leaving appointments angry, frustrated, and let down, and no nearer to getting the help their child needed. Children and teenagers can leave these appointments emotionally fragile with their hopes taken away. In the third session, once again the psychotherapist asked Jon about his role play in childhood. 'Tell me about the dinosaurs,' he said. I thought, *enough now with the Freudian bullshit!* and felt myself getting angrier and angrier. Jon responded to him mimicking the same professional tone – 'Tell me what is it about you and these dinosaurs, I think you are starting to get a little obsessed with them!' Bullshit over, we spent the rest of the session trying to get some clear answers to our questions on a treatment plan, having made it plain that the time for dinosaurs was over. We were told that there was a long waiting list (six months to a year) before even commencing any possible treatment. We left that final session feeling totally unsupported and let down.

Given the feedback from so many parents on their lack of progress with the Tavi we had already looked ahead into any private options that were available in the UK. Dr Richard Curtis was recommended at Transhealth, the London gender clinic, which is the largest private transgender clinic in the UK.

We both knew that waiting for treatment via the NHS was not an option. Nat was honest with me and said that she did not think she would be able to make it through if she had to wait that long. Emotionally she was very low, her female puberty adding to that turmoil. I know parents who have had to be on 24/7 suicide watch with their transgender children because of the agonisingly long waiting lists. Suicide rates for transgender kids are high, so is self-harming. There are not enough NHS medical resources and services available in the UK to provide the support and treatment that is so desperately needed. Parents struggle, their children struggle and the outcome of this struggle can be (and has been) the tragic loss of your child. I made the decision to go private and I have never regretted that choice, it was the right thing to do. I was not going to lose my child.

I made an appointment with Dr Curtis. Nat really worried about the money side of things, knowing that as a single working parent finances were always tight. I reassured her that what was most important was her well-being and transition and that the financial side was my concern only (it would, in fact, make a substantial dent in my budget but I had no choice, we had no choice). We both felt buoyed up when we came out of Dr Curtis's office. Here was a professional who fully understood my child's condition and who was willing to discuss the possibilities of treatment. His decisions were carefully considered, grounded in Nat's past history of depression, the counselling she had received, her progress so far on her journey of transitioning and, most importantly, Nat herself. As preparation for her appointment we had faxed through pages that she had written. In them she expressed her feelings on her gender dysphoria, her knowledge and understanding of the transition process she wanted to undertake and how her life felt at that point. Nat had sat opposite Dr Curtis and I sat on the sofa, which was placed away from his desk and patient. He addressed Nat and only very occasionally did I interrupt by asking a question. This appointment was about my child.

The next step was for Nat to have blood tests to check her hormone levels before any treatment could be considered, so our GP had these done. A month later we had our second appointment with Dr Curtis. We both left his office elated.

Nat was to have Hormone Replacement Therapy. She was now at last on a treatment plan. She was sixteen and did not have to wait another two agonising years. Our GP put in place the funding for her testosterone therapy; he had battled with the local Primary Care Trust to get this. If it wasn't for his professional support and care I would have had to finance this too (how I do not know, but again there would have been no choice, I would somehow have to do it). We would continue to have private follow-up appointments with Dr Curtis during the treatment, these we would have to pay for. My financial commitment was nothing compared to parents I knew who had to re-mortgage or take out loans to pay for treatment abroad because their child's situation was becoming unbearable and they were too young to be considered for any treatment in the UK.

Natasha could now begin her journey of physical transition to being Jonathan.

Nine

The End of the Beginning

Jon: The happiness of being me

I'm writing this in December 2012. I'm a pagan, and it's a traditional time of year to reflect on all the good that's happened to me over the course of my transition, and all that's made my journey challenging. One word I would use to describe my transition would be lucky. Two words: very lucky.

I recently went to Spain, after four years of not seeing my family, now as Jon ('Juan'), with a beard, as opposed to a 'moony' face and bushy curly hair. The reaction was phenomenal; when the documentary was released in 2009, my mother told them about my transition (they have not seen the documentary yet and I am hoping that it is aired in a Spanish-speaking country, so we will be able to get a copy of the subtitled or dubbed version so they can see it), but seeing them physically accept me – the men shake my hand, the smiles, the hugs – made me realise that I had such an accepting family. They didn't just tolerate my transition, they love me still as a person. A new person, but still the young nephew or cousin they remembered from my teen days at my cousin's wedding. I don't speak Spanish, and my mum translated dinner table conversation from gesticulating rapid-paced Spanish conversations into English. She said when we came back from Spain, that everyone thought I was 'brave'. I don't see it myself, and this isn't me trying to be all humble, I just went with it (might have been a bonus that I didn't speak Spanish though!), going with the flow is what I tend to do. I just expected them, as decent people, to have a decent reaction to me. And also, that word again – luck – was on my side. I know some families that aren't as accepting, on the other hand I know some wonderful families. My family has been accepting and understanding from the start. For that, for fate, I'm eternally grateful. I haven't explained anything to them, I haven't pleaded or bargained with them. They've just 'got it'; and that's a rare thing.

From the moment I came out, I believe I've had it good. I've not been made homeless, as so many young trans people are; I haven't been subject to physical or emotional violence from family members because of it. I even didn't have that bad a school experience, despite all my tribulations and the obvious bullying. Maybe I'm playing it down again. But I prefer to focus on the here and now. Once you live a few more months, a year, two years, time takes the edge off things. I don't often think back to the past. I'm focused on what my gender is bringing me now, and if something from the past is niggling me, I will sort it out. All of the bad stuff that happened to me from other people was at school, and I have left now, free to make my way as I choose without the baggage of people who 'knew me before'.

Everything I have gone through, the good and the bad, has made me grow. My experiences, with school, coming out, changing my name, and transitioning physically have helped other people. In the trans community, knowledge is handed down. Everything I've found out, I've found out from other people, many of whom became my friends. They're the ones who supplied me with the armour I needed when I went back to school, and who provided me with a space where I could talk. Being in the good situation I'm in with transition allowed me to appreciate my life for what it was when things got tough: I know it wasn't as bad as it could have been. I think that's what defines my transition for me: it's a story that was positive from the beginning, and it shows that transition can be a good experience, if people are understanding.

I don't think I'm particularly different from most other people my age, and not that much different to other trans young people. From the outside, as my mum said to me, the trans community is a 'whole new world', but from the inside, it's very much a small group. Interesting at times, same-old at times, with the same people, and same spaces. It's like a little village. Or maybe 'village' is too comfortable and cute a word. But if you go to a trans event, or a queer event in your region, it's likely that you'll know someone, or know someone who knows someone. I've been recognised a few times at FtM meets and once outside Dr Curtis's office (I've got the kind of face that nobody can quite place, but most people know they've seen me on the telly).

My experiences have made me think a lot more than if I hadn't been trans. I've thought a lot more about gender and society, and about society in general, and sexism and feminism, all linking on from my immersion in trans protests and queer events, and through reading other people's writings on their own gender theories and experiences. It's definitely made me a rounded person, and I'm glad for this shot of maturity and understanding. In my journey, I've tried to help others as much as I can with their issues, especially if they were the same things I was going through. I remember talking with many people about appointments at the NHS gender clinic, and different doctors; I still do – I like to keep on top of what's happening, even after I've received my hormones. I still love to talk about gender. It fascinates me, and I am always exploring new sides to it and new ways to express myself. I would like people to continue to watch my documentary as a starting point, but to also 'go with the flow' themselves and remember that not one path is for everyone. One lesson that's important to remember, especially for young trans people faced with a massive amount of information, is that there is no one way to be trans, and no one can tell you how you should feel in your own situation. That it's good to experiment, good to explore and good to change and rediscover things. This attitude is what made me feel comfortable in going through transition so young. That I had time to think, and a bright future ahead of me.

People often want to know if I have made the right decision, if I will regret it. And I think that's the most common thing trans people who are undergoing transition are asked: what will it be like in the future?

I'm not nearly enough 'in the future' to talk about how it is in the future (I'm only twenty! Come back to me in a couple of decades). So I cannot answer this question. Nobody can. Of course the default answer is, yes this is the right decision, but no one can be sure. Judging from how I felt pre-transition and judging on how I am feeling now, this is the path that I want (read, need) to be on. So - do I feel comfortable in my own skin at the present time, if this is the way I look at it? Am I now completely satisfied?

The answer of course is no, and not because of not having had *xyz* operation. My physical appearance is still evolving, and will take a few more years on testosterone to change. I wish my beard was a bit more even, I wish my skin wasn't as greasy, all those trivial everyday things cis and trans people share alike about their appearance as they go through puberty and mature into adults. I am waiting to be comfortable in my own skin. A snake will only stop shedding its skin when it's dead; for me there is a great deal of living to do before that.

My appearance constantly changes, as does my gender identity. Sometimes those two will interlink. If I'm having a bad day I might want to shave or bind or wear different clothes, which in turn makes me explore how I am presenting my gender. I've been exploring gender roles throughout transition, and I will continue to do this as long as I still identify as 'trans'. My gender will always be something I am conscious about, something that will remain in the forefront of my mind, and will affect me in many ways, good and bad. Whether or not I decide to have specific surgeries in the future will depend on how I view myself in the future. At the moment, I'm happy enough to have small breasts and to wait for surgery; I'm not in a huge rush. In the future though, would I want to settle down as 'just a guy'? Will I forget all of this, as my gender unfolds again? Why shouldn't it?

However, gender fluidity is my past, and I believe my love of combining feminine and masculine elements and destroying the gender binary will be part of my future. I can't see a future as a 'traditional' male, there's just so much more to gender than a simple transition from one to the other for me. Everything about my personal transition is growth and evolution. Gender is in my mind.

So no, I am not comfortable in my own skin. Very few people are, so one cannot expect a trans person to be comfortable, especially after a history of dysphoria, doubt and body issues.

My relationship with my mum hasn't changed throughout my transition. She's always been someone who I could rely on to be stronger than me, to have all the answers. She's always been understanding, and always been there for me, too. Even though she suffers from bipolar, the good times make me forget the bad, and when I look at her I always think, 'How can she ever be anything but a rock for me?' I've really never seen her upset or angry because of anything do to with my gender identity, only concern for me. Again, I've been so lucky.

She's made a new social group, made up of families of young trans and queer people, through my gender identity experience, so I think this has been good for her as well as me. She's part of a PFLAG(T) network – a group for parents and friends of LGBTQ people in London, and although she's the only parent there with a trans child, it seems to help. She talks a lot to other parents about her experiences, and comes to trans events to help other parents. She has never been ashamed of me. The one thing she's always been is proud, proud of me and my achievements. Never once has my sexuality or gender identity been a source of shame or disappointment to her, even though it may have been to me. She's always put me first. Any prospective partner she had, she always made sure that they were 100 per cent okay with me being trans and queer, and if not, that was the end of that.

She could have lost her family in coming out for me. Luckily, that wasn't the case, but she could have decided to do the thing that a lot of parents do and keep quiet, hoping to never have to bring 'it' up with that side of the family. But I was more important to her than that.

Even though non-trans people can't ever fully understand what being trans is like, she has accepted this, and I know that I can always talk to her if I needed to. I never really have gone to her with my gender troubles, but the option was there.

Having a mum that's been so understanding and accepting throughout your life, you never really appreciate how good she is until other people make you aware of it. It's just something you expect.

But thanks, Mum, for everything.

Where do I see myself going? To be honest I'm not sure. I'm only twenty and have my whole life ahead of me. This is merely the end of the beginning of my life and there are loads of things I want to do. I'd like to travel more. I have a phobia of flying, so that might be a difficulty, but I've always wanted to go to New Zealand and Finland. In terms of future transition – I'd like to roll with that. I've got no 'plans'; I can't 'plan' how my gender will form in years to come, or if there will be any change at all and I will simply remain Jon. But I'd like to ultimately continue to live a life true to myself, and eventually die surrounded by my children and cats and family – respected, and loved by the people who knew me. Gender, whilst a defining factor throughout your life, when you get to the end of the end it doesn't matter. I just want the happiness of being me.

Luisa: Dear Jon

Dear Jon

My final chapter is for you. These words are yours. I want you to know and remember them when your journey in life is difficult. They are what is essential, and when you remember them and hold on to them I hope that they will help see you through times of pain.

When you were born and I held you in my arms for that first time, I fell in love with you. You have always been a gift to me, an essential part of my heart and soul.

You have made me a better person and mother. You have taught me so much. How to become the person that we all have the right to be. Your courage has inspired me and shown me that against many odds we can always make our choice to be the individual that we are. That each and every living being is what is most important. It is a privilege to know and have you as my child. I thank you for that.

Remember always that your courage, your integrity has made my life a wonderful and extraordinary experience. If I was given the choice to make changes in my life, I would make none.

'To the ocean and back.' I have loved and will always love you because you are my precious child and because you are the person that you are today.

Always,

Mum

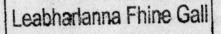

Resources

Families Together London
London-based LGBTQ support group
www.familiestogetherlondon.com
Tel: 07806 746780 or 020 8874 4214
Email: hatta@familiestogetherlondon.com

Gendered Intelligence (GI)
Understanding gender diversity in creative ways
www.genderedintelligence.co.uk

Gender Identity Research and Education Society (GIRES)
Information for trans people, their families and the
professionals who care for them

www.gires.org.uk
Address: Melverley, The Warren, Ashtead, Surrey,
KT21 2SP
Tel: 01372 801554
Email: info@gires.org.uk

Mermaids
Family and individual support for teenagers and
children with gender identity issues
www.mermaidsuk.org.uk
Address: BM Mermaids, London, WC1N 3XX
Tel: 020 8123 4819
Email: info@mermaidsuk.org.uk

PACE
London-based support group promoting the mental
health and emotional well-being of the lesbian, gay,
bisexual and transgender community
www.pacehealth.org.uk
Address: 34 Hartham Road, London, N7 9JL
Tel: 020 7700 1323
Email: info@pacehealth.org.uk

PFLAG(T) network
US-based support group for LGBTQ people
www.community.pflag.org
Address: 1828 L Street, NW, Suite 660, Washington

DC 20036, USA
Tel: 001 (202) 467-8180
Email: info@pflag.org

Press for Change
Experts in transgender law
www.pfc.org.uk
Address: BM Network, London, WC1N 3XX
Tel: 08448 708165
Email: office@pfc.org.uk

The Gender Identity Clinic (GIC) (sometimes known
as the Charing Cross GIC)
Support and advice in transgender issues
www.wlmht.nhs.uk/gi/gender-identity-clinic/
Address: 179–183 Fulham Palace Road, London,
W6 8QZ
Tel: 020 8483 2801

**The Tavistock and Portman NHS Foundation
Trust**
Gender identity development service
www.tavi-port.org
Address: Tavistock Centre, 120 Belsize Lane,
London, NW3 5BA
Tel: 020 7435 7111

QYN (Queer Youth Network)
A youth group for LGBTQ and queer young people
www.queeryouth.org.uk
Tel: 07092 031086
Email: info@queryouth.net

Glossary

androgyne: neither male nor female; rather a combination of both, or a state of being neither (commonly referred to as being *agender*). A person may use this term how they wish.

bigender: being male and female, either at the same time or fluctuating.

binary gender system/binary gender: the system that only has male and female as gender options.

cis: people who are happy that the sex assigned to them at birth matches their mental gender.

cissexist/cissexism: the belief that the genders of trans people are less legitimate than those of cis gender people.

genderbend: transcend gender norms. Also called genderfucking.

gender dysphoria: acute feeling of mismatch between the sex assigned to you at birth and your gender. Gender Identity Disorder is a formal diagnosis.

genderqueer: an identification that a person who is not binary gendered may use. This can encompass a range of gender identities and expressions, and is used as an umbrella term for those with a non-binary gender.

going stealth: not being out as transgender.

HRT (hormone replacement therapy): hormone treatment as a form of medical transition; testosterone or oestrogen.

LGBT: Lesbian, Gay, Bisexual and Transgender.

LGBTQ: Lesbian, Gay, Bisexual, Transgender and Queer.

non-binary: not fitting into the gender binary of exclusively male or female.

pansexual: having the capacity to be attracted to all genders.

transgender: an umbrella definition to describe individuals whose gender identity and/or sex identity does not match the one they were assigned at birth.

trans: an umbrella definition that includes binary transgender people (trans women and trans men) and non-binary trans identities (genderqueer, bigender, etc.).

transsexual: a person may identify as transsexual if they have taken medical procedures to feel comfortable within their gender identity and/or sex identity.

transphobia: the fear or hatred of trans people.